GW00729141

David Fountain is a writer, photographer and artist who has travelled far and wide on several different motorcycles. Join him on his adventures in France, Spain, Portugal, Ireland, Scandinavia, Germany, Australia (without a bike) and the UK. Meet many interesting people such as Catholic priests on retreat at Buckfast Abbey and the young German whose grandfather was a fighter pilot and who apologised to David on behalf of Herr Hitler for dumping huge bombs in the Thames Estuary and almost knocking his mum off her bike as she cycled to work at RAF Intelligence during the war.

To Paul ~

THE ART OF PACKING

David Fountain

Dave

_I hope you enjoy
reading this as
much as I enjoyed
writing it._

First published in 2018.

© Copyright David Fountain 2018.

The moral right of David Fountain to be identified as the author of this work has been asserted by him in accordance with the Copyright Designs and Patents Act 1988.

All rights reserved. No part of this publication may be reproduced or transmitted in any form or by any means, electronic or mechanical, including photocopying, recording or any information storage or retrieval system, without either prior permission in writing from the publisher or a license permitting restricted use in the United Kingdom or United States. Such licenses are issued by the Copyright Licensing Agency, 90 Tottenham Court Road, London W1P 0LP.

All photographs © David Fountain.

Cover design © David Fountain 2018.

The author can be contacted by email to:-
davidjohnelroro@gmail.com

ISBN 978-1-717-52629-8

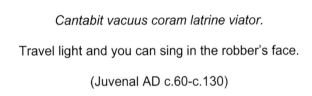

Cantabit vacuus coram latrine viator.

Travel light and you can sing in the robber's face.

(Juvenal AD c.60-c.130)

The Art of Packing

All the stuff I took on a trip to France. For scale see helmet, bottom left.

TRAVELLERS TIP - It's a Law of the Universe that your possessions expand to fill the space available and it's well worth remembering this as you pack. If you don't then your bags will end up stuffed to capacity and zips could burst apart all over the place. In any case it's a good idea to have a bit of spare capacity in case you acquire any interesting things on your travels.

When packing, what you need to do is make three piles of stuff - essential, desirable and might be able to do without. Leave the last pile at home. You will be able to do without that stuff.

Next, be ruthless with the middle pile. Think about each item in turn. Ask yourself if you really need it. If the answer is 'well actually I could probably do without it, and it is something I could probably buy when I'm away anyway' then definitely leave it at home.

Lastly, have a ruthless look at your essentials just to check that all that stuff really is essential. Weed out anything that isn't.

If you apply these checks to your luggage you will be able to reduce the volume and weight considerably.

All the stuff packed away. The bike is my beautiful Honda CB1000R which started life as Dragon Green but I had it sprayed red. It's the best bike I've ever had, better even than my Norton Dominator 600.

France, August 2008

Six of us with six bikes arrive at Folkstone for the Eurotunnel train. We're heading for the Black Forest and possibly beyond. Within a few minutes we're on a train speeding through the seabed on its way to France.

A few tunnel facts:-

Speeding trains act like pistons and cause a build-up of air pressure in front of the train. Ducts connecting the two main tunnels allow pressure to be released.

If fire breaks out inside a train, the driver mustn't stop but must complete the journey and the train is received into a special fire bay at the terminal.

The UK increased in size by ninety acres due to deposits of tunnel spoil. The extra bit of land is now used for walking, fishing and picnicking.

Driving on the other side of the road is pretty strange if, like me, you've never done it before, and driving anticlockwise round a roundabout feels positively illegal. Overnight many years ago the Swedes switched to driving on the right to bring themselves into line with all other European countries (except the UK). An impressive achievement.

Our line of six motorcycles soon develops a pecking order of riding positions but I'm not sure where I should be and end up trailing in final position. Approaching Le Touquet I somehow get left behind and find myself on a very small road lost in a wood. I see a woman on a bicycle stopped at a junction. Her hair is almost as red as her anorak. I pull up alongside her and stop the engine. She speaks no English at all. I dredge up some French from the distant past and we manage an inadequate conversation. Once we've established that I don't want to play golf or go for a walk in the woods, I manage to communicate that I'm looking for my companions who will in all probability be eating nearby. She points me in the direction of the seafront cafés and sure enough that's where I find them.

The menu advertises Welsh Rarebit and I order some. It turns out to be a piece of bread marooned inside a bowlful of melted orange cheese, all of it floating on a lake of olive oil. I lose my appetite.

On the road to Saint Quentin (san-con-tan) a split develops in our group of six. Three want to speed off to Germany according to a strict itinerary, and the other three of us are more relaxed about the whole thing and want to leave a bit of space to hang about in interesting places if it takes our fancy to do so. I don't think it was ever really on the cards keeping six people together on a trip like this. Different people want to do different things. Trevor, George and I (the less hasty contingent) stop on the outskirts of Saint Quentin and make the mistake of asking a drunk old man *'Monsieur, ou est le camping, s'il vous plâit?'* First he points one way, then the other. He clearly doesn't know the location of the camping. A jogger in an orange tracksuit appears on the other side of the road. We attract his attention and he jogs over to us and continues to jog on the spot. He's a little more help and we deduce that le camping is a kilometre or two down the road and off somewhere to the left. The jogger puts himself in gear and jogs off. The drunk old man becomes animated and flings his arms around in wild gestures but we don't understand what he's trying to tell us.

We find le camping eventually but by then it's pouring with rain, the entrance gate is locked and I find out through an intercom that there are no vacancies anyway.

We head for the centre of town and find a magnificent hotel with, it seems, all its rooms available. We each take a double.

Monday August 25th

I've stopped at a church on the edge of Rheims. I saw a big circular window at the front and went to look inside. There's a couple of inebriated men slumped by the entrance door. They look harmless enough and too drunk to carry out any criminal activity, but I take my luggage inside just in case. As I'm unstrapping my bags Trevor and George ride past without seeing me. The moment has a dream-like quality and I feel I want to run after them. It's my fault they've gone past - I said I'd meet them at the cathedral but I've been sidetracked.

As I enter the church I realise it's a very special place.

The stained glass windows are astonishingly beautiful and cast exquisite patterns on the walls and floor. There are life-size wooden carvings of Jesus and Mary, mounted on stone plinths. Both have been severely infested with woodworm (especially round the knees for some reason), but this hasn't detracted from

Church on the edge of Rheims.

the superb quality of the carving. The folds in Jesus's cloak are divine in every sense.

There's a marble plaque which can be loosely translated as, 'In this place remember the ones who died to give us victory and peace'.

Tuesday August 26th

It's afternoon and I arrive at the campsite just off the Sacred Road which leads into Verdun from the west. It got its name in World War One because it was the only road along which supplies could be brought to support the horrible battle which took place around this town.

For le camping I'm given Plot 137 which is slightly sloping and rather close to a railway line but on the plus side is well away from all the motor homes and has a small tree with a branch stub which looks to be a perfect peg on which to hang a wet towel or jacket. On closer examination though, the tree is full of very ripe pears which appear to have the potential to drop steadily onto any tent pitched below.

I get my tent sorted out (well away from the pear tree) and go for a wander.

TRAVELLERS TIP - When buying a tent bear in mind that storage space is useful space - especially the bit outside the inner tent but under cover of the fly sheet. If you're on your own then you'd be better off with a tent designed to sleep two to give yourself some extra storage space. If there's two of you then it's worth considering a tent designed to sleep three or even four. That extra space makes tent-dwelling a lot more comfortable.

Another thing to consider is how easy the tent is to put up and take down. If it's dark or wet you'll be really glad you bought the one that can be put up in five minutes rather than the one that takes half an hour. These days many tents pretty well put themselves up by springing into shape once removed from their container.

This is a pretty upmarket campsite. There's a bar, free internet access and a terrace with tables and chairs. The shop looks well stocked and outside there's a magnificent swimming pool with water as blue as a tropical lagoon and a water chute to slide down. In the bar there's a small library of books that people have left behind for others to read. That's always a useful facility.

I cook up a sauce with some chopped red pepper, mushrooms and green beans and have that with a chunk of baguette and a cup of tea. After that it's nearly dark and I turn in for the night. I discover that if I spend a couple of minutes winding up my new LED head light (which can be attached to my head with elastic straps) then I'll have enough light for about twenty minutes before it needs winding again. That seems a good enough return for a couple of minutes winding.

Wednesday August 27th

Very early am

It's not light yet. Pears are dropping and bouncing outside with clockwork regularity. Amazing how loud that sounds in the middle of the night, but at least I'm not camped under the tree.

A bit later

It's only just light. A seemingly endless train pulled by a diesel engine rumbles past and shakes the campsite. A Frenchman later tells me that this is the only train of the day and it carries some kind of white powder for local industrial use.

TRAVELLERS TIP - Pack a few pairs of ear plugs to keep out sounds of falling pears, diesel trains, irritating children and anything else you don't want to hear.

Early afternoon

I have a neighbor. He's moving in to Plot 138. Bushes divide our two plots. He's a young guy with an old Yamaha single cylinder 600cc off-road motor bike. I walk down to the shop to buy some milk and when I get back I light my stove and offer the man from 138 some coffee. He accepts and provides a rather posh stainless steel mug and I'm immediately jealous and make a mental not to buy a similar one. I forgot to bring a mug and I've been using a mushroom soup tin with the lid removed, but it's not the most practical of drinking vessels because it's too hot to hold.

My new neighbour is a young German guy called Peter Hessel

from Münster and he's returning home after travelling round the south of France and southern Spain before starting in October at the Westfälische Wilhelms Universität to study history and archaeology (he tells me the university was named in honour of Kaiser Wilhelm 1st). We get on with each other straight away. I have a theory that the least likely place you will find people you get on with is within your own family, and the most likely place is on the road when you're travelling.

Peter Hessel on his old Yamaha wearing my false beard (in my opinion an essential travelling accessory).

Peter is twenty-one, tall, blond and short-haired. After leaving school he decided he wanted to spend his working life fixing motorcycles and he worked as an apprentice mechanic at a Harley Davidson shop. They promised him a proper contract but it never materialised and he left after a year but nonetheless had acquired a good working knowledge of motorcycle mechanics. Before setting out on this trip he bought two ex SAS British Army steel ammunition boxes and made up a welded frame to attach them to his bike.

Peter has a wonderful disrespect for authority and sense of rebellion. He tells me that young Germans have to do a spell of military service or community work and he chose the latter but it was still a bit military in its organisation. They told him he was to work in an old people's home but he refused, saying that it didn't suit his nature. They didn't like his attitude but agreed to place him elsewhere.

Peter says in some ways he regrets not taking the army option because he would have liked the shooting and the explosions and all the fun things to do, but he says he would never go to war. He'd remain neutral like Holland or Switzerland.

He tells me his two favourite books about the First World War are *All Quiet On The Western Front* by Erich Remarque (one of my favourite books too - the story is told by a German soldier, but he could just as easily have been on the other side). Peter says his other favourite is *The Way Back* also by Erich Remarque, which tells how survivors returned from the war, crippled and traumatized and couldn't understand why society wasn't interested in them any more.

TRAVELLER'S TIP - Use string for a washing line. Tie one end to something, twist two lengths tightly together then tie the other end to something else. Make openings in the twists to insert your washing. It'll hold it better than pegs.

PETER'S HISTORY LESSON (in his own words) - In 1870 France and Germany were not on speaking term and France declared war on Germany. At the time His Imperial and Royal Majesty Wilhelm the First was King of Prussia and the first German emperor. He wasn't too keen on having wars but thought he'd better join in anyway. Germany won the war and took some land as a reward. This annoyed France no end.

By 1914 a lot of countries in Europe weren't getting on well with each other. Kaiser Wilhelm the Second was in charge of Germany. He had an army called the Kaiserliche and they all wore funny helmets with spikes. The Kaiser's helmet had a bird sitting on it so that was the funniest of all. In June 1914 the Archduke Franz

Ferdinand (heir apparent to the Austro-Hungarian throne) was having a break in Sarajevo (a town in Bosnia) with his wife Sophie where he opened a museum. A young Bosnian fellow called Gavrilo Princip didn't like Mr Ferdinand at all so he shot him and his wife and killed them both. This made a lot of people unhappy so they started the First World War and all together twenty million people died and another twenty million were injured. Germany got blamed for the war and the Kaiser was told he could no longer be Kaiser but he never really got used to the idea and he went to live in a big house in Holland called Haus Doorn and spent the rest of his life angrily chopping wood. Wilhelm was Queen Victoria's grandson and she was possibly the only person in the world (apart from his mum maybe) who thought much of him, although had she known what he'd get up to a few years after her death she might have gone off him.

About twenty-one years later in 1939 an Austrian chap living in Germany called Adolf Hitler invaded Poland. This made a lot of people unhappy so they started the Second World War. Herr Hitler was a difficult man. He'd wanted to be an artist but he was very bad at painting so he thought he'd become an evil dictator instead, which gave him the opportunity to ban all art that didn't depict wholesome scenes and family values (his kind of art). He put all the pictures he didn't like in an exhibition of 'Degenerate Art' and banned the artists from painting any more pictures, but fortunately some of them ignored him. Herr Hitler was completely off his trolley but was a bit clever too and a few years earlier had made himself quite popular by offering the German people what they wanted - Autobahns, employment and Volkswagens.

Herr Hitler had been a lowly soldier during World War One and was looked upon with contempt by many of the senior officers in the Wehrmacht (army, literally, defence force). Herr Hitler lost the war, but, like Kaiser Wilhelm the Second, he was a bad loser (as well as a bad artist) and couldn't come to terms with the idea that the enemy had won. He became very fed up and didn't fancy the idea of being executed by anybody else so he poisoned his dog, his wife and himself with cyanide, and, to make sure he was properly dead, shot himself in the head as well. So it turned out that not only was Herr Hitler a bad artist and a bad loser, but he was also a bad dog owner, a bad husband and a bad dictator ... but a good shot, at least at close range.

TRAVELLER'S TIP - Leave some space in your luggage to take a few interesting things home with you. I use most of the things I take but could survive with less.

BATTLE OF VERDUN

When die Kaiserliche invaded Verdun in 1914 it resulted in one of the biggest battles of all time - 300 days and 300 nights of fierce fighting with the French managing to hold Verdun itself throughout, but the toll was huge on both sides. The Germans managed an advance of only a few kilometres from the original front line.

Douament Fort, melted gun emplacement.

In those few months something like half a million died and up to 300,000 were injured (estimates vary). Young men, old men, women, children, pets, cows, sheep, horses in the fields all died or were injured.

The conditions were appalling for both sides. Mud, constant shelling with huge German artillery - a million shells fell just within the first few hours. So much changed because of war - families were decimated (everyone in the town lost at least one family member and many families were entirely wiped out). The landscape itself was also changed for ever - shelling decimated whole swathes of trees and created its own strange landscapes; in time the shell craters became soft and grassy and transformed into open areas of undulating hillocks. The largest German guns used 400mm shells (each shell as tall as a man with the girth of a mature tree trunk) and the devastation they caused is visible to this day. The shelling was so intense that the shell craters joined up with each other.

War graves at Douamont

They were miserable wretches on both sides. Cold, badly fed and under constant and extremely heavy attack, many were made mad. At times it snowed. Their injuries were horrible. The sheer number of deaths alone - whether strangers, relatives, friends or new acquaintances must have been enough to make their daily lives full of paranoia, fear and despair. The longing to be home, whichever side you were on, must have been huge.

I saw a photo of a French soldier on leave in 1916. He is filthy, exhausted and shell-shocked. I think it can safely be said he had no desire to return to the battle of Verdun. Perhaps he survived the next two years, or perhaps he was one of the unlucky (or maybe lucky) ones who didn't make it. Many must have wished themselves dead, such was the hell of Verdun.

AT THE DOCTORS

Ah Madame, j'ai besoin d'un docteur pour le medicament parce que je suis fou - j'ai perdu mes comprimés. Combien pour voyer un docteur, s'il vous plâit?

It takes me ages to come up with this sentence which, roughly translated, means 'I'm an idiot, I've lost my tablets, how much to see a doctor, please?'

The doctor turns out to speak perfect English and with no fuss prescribes me what I need.

Douamont, shell craters.

THE THIRD REICH

Talking with Peter about the Third Reich reminds me that I have a couple of complaints relating to Germany's part in the War and seeing as he's the nearest German he might have a bit of apologising to do.

Firstly I tell him that one day during the War my mum was cycling home from her work as a shorthand typist for RAF Intelligence. She would have been in her blue uniform and must have been about seventeen or eighteen. She heard the motor of a V2 rocket (a Doodlebug) cut out overhead. A bit later there was a huge explosion at the end of the road and she nearly fell off her bike.

"I'm very sorry", says Peter, *"I can only apologise on behalf of the Luftwaffe."*

"I accept your apology, Peter. Thank you very much." We shake hands in a very gentlemanly manner.

"And your other complaint about my country's part in the War?"

"Ah yes, that concerns my friend Nigel who is a fisherman working mainly in the Thames Estuary. One day he was out in his boat and something very heavy got caught in his net. Unable to haul it in and being reluctant to cut the net loose, he dragged it in, bumping along the bottom, to the shore. In shallow water he saw it was a massive bomb. He called the coastguard who in turn alerted the bomb disposal unit who arrived as soon as possible. It turned out it was a twelve foot long parachute bomb which were sensitive to the vibrations of ship's engines. They were designed to lay on the bottom of the sea and allow a certain number of ships to pass over them before exploding. The bomb disposal chaps took it back out to sea and exploded it, sending a huge plume of water into the air.

"Your lot could have blown up my friend and severely damaged the town I live in", I complain to Peter.

"Once again, I am very sorry for the inconvenience it caused your friend and the British Army. I can only apologise once again on behalf of the Luftwaffe and the German people."

That's ok, it wasn't your fault. No hard feelings."

Once again we shake hands.

Peter's grandfather, Josef Hessel, flew Focke Wolf FW-190 fighters in World War Two on strategic bombing missions. He was qualified to fly Heinkel bombers and all other German warplanes of the time. When the war ended he did private flying work until he was in his seventies. He's now eighty-seven and re-tells the same war stories again and again at every opportunity. Family members do their best to listen politely and respectfully at any gatherings where the old man is present.

He had four brothers, one of whom was also a Luftwaffe pilot who flew missions to where the Germans were fighting the Russians. He had a wooden stick and would carve a star into it to represent each Russian plane he shot down. One day when returning from a mission he bumped his head inside the cockpit on landing and suffered concussion and confusion. Almost straight away he was sent on another mission and never returned. When the Luftwaffe packed his things in a box to be returned to his family the stick was too long to fit in the box and they cut off part of it and just sent the main part, which had thirty-eight stars carved into it. The family never knew how many enemy aircraft he really shot down.

TRAVELLER'S TIP - If your motorcycle gloves are not waterproof (or have lost their waterproofing), buy a few pairs of cheap plastic gloves (the sort mechanics use to protect their hands from grease and oil, and doctors use for sticking their fingers up bottoms). Wear them under your non-waterproof gloves and keep your hands dry (if maybe a bit sweaty, but talc can help with that).

WAITING FOR A LAVABO

One morning at the campsite I go to the shower block with the washbasins early so as to avoid the rush. It's not even seven o'clock but every one of the six basins is occupied, each by a young man in camouflage trousers and no top. Each man is shaving.

As I wait, more young men in military gear come in and form a queue behind me. From the small black, yellow and red flag on each man's uniform I realise they are German soldiers and I remember seeing some military vehicles making their way to Verdun the day before. They must have been heading for this campsite.

My turn at the lavabo arrives and as I wash, more soldiers arrive and wait in line for free basins. I can see them in the mirror. As I

Early morning, Verdun campsite.

leave I say, *"Good morning, good morning , good morning"* to the three soldiers by the exit, but none replies.

Outside I say to a soldier, *"Are you from the German Army?"* He fetches another soldier who speaks good English.

He tells me that all the young men are doing their national service (choosing the Army over social work) and one of the conditions is that they visit Verdun and other battle grounds in order to understand what happened there less than a hundred years ago. Today his group is to visit the Citadel which he says has an excellent tour.

TRAVELLER'S TIP - If you're not a photographer, don't worry - buy postcards instead and end up with a bunch of professionally taken photos. If you've got no scruples you might even be able to convince friends and relatives you took them yourself.

MY BIKE GETS DAMAGED

It's ten o'clock at night. The campsite is quiet. I fancy a bottle of Heineken beer but the campsite bar is shut. No problem - I'll take my bike into town and get one there.

As I approach the exit to the campsite I see that a massive steel gate has been pulled across and locked. I swing the bike around to return to my tent but I'm going so slowly that I need to put my foot down to steady myself. In the dark I don't see that the ground slopes away steeply and there's nothing to support my foot. I lose my balance and the bike begins to tip. I try to stop it but it's a dead weight so I let go and jump out of the way.

The silence of the campsite is shattered by the sound of plastic breaking and metal crashing onto the road.

People come out of their tents and motorhomes. They must think there's been a catastrophe.

The manager comes out of the reception building and helps me lift the bike upright. I try to start it but the engine won't turn over. It seems the fall has damaged the engine. A mirror has snapped off completely and skidded across the road. One of the indicators is hanging off. I'm sure the engine casings will be badly scratched.

I feel very vulnerable in this corner of France with a broken bike, a fair bit of luggage and no way home.

The following day I'm up at dawn to assess the damage.

There's a broken mirror and indicator, a deeply scratched silencer heat shield, scratched engine casings and one handlebar end worn away a bit. Fortunately it's all fixable or cosmetic.

About eight o'clock I make a call to the breakdown people and within an hour a chirpy Frenchman arrives with his brand new rescue truck. It's so new that the motorcycle securing kit is still wrapped in plastic. We strap the bike on the back and he takes me to a nearby motorcycle dealer with a big workshop.

A few minutes later I'm hanging around the showroom waiting for an assessment from the mechanics when I hear my bike roar into life. It seems the impact jammed the starter motor. Nothing more serious than that.

Things get better. They tell me it's all fixable and it should be ready by four o'clock.

One of the mechanics gives me a lift to the campsite in his car.

I return to the bike shop at four o'clock and pick up the bike. I'm very relieved that I can continue my trip.

It turns out the new indicators flash twice as fast as the old ones and the mirrors are more flimsy than the originals (in fact so flimsy that wind pressure makes them fold into the bike at speed), but what the heck, I thought it was the end of my adventure but I'm on my way again.

THE HUN

I ask Peter how the Germans became to be known as The Hun. His explanation was as follows.

"Kaiser Wilhelm the Second (Queen Victoria's grandson, who was possibly the only person in the world who loved him dearly) gave a famous speech in which he encouraged his army to attack the enemy with the same gusto as did Attila the Hun. It was this speech which caused the German armies of both the Second (Wilhelm's Kaiserliche) and Third (Hitler's Wehrmacht) Reich to be disparagingly known as The Hun. The Hun were ruthless warriors who would stop at nothing to achieve the objectives of their leader Attila."

TRAVELLER'S TIP

When packing your clothes, don' t fold them, roll them up. Shirts, t-shirts, underwear, jumpers, trousers can all be tightly rolled. You'll find they'll stuff better into small spaces and when you unroll them they won't be nearly as creased as they would be if you'd folded them.

THE CITADEL AT VERDUN

The citadel at Verdun penetrates deep into the bedrock and the underground passages are many kilometres long. It was built in the mid-nineteenth century and during the First World War was an important base for the French military involved in the defence of Verdun.

Wide passages were converted into hospital wards, dormitories, living quarters, chapels and stores. Deep underground a lack of ventilation meant that the air was often foul, but at least the place was safe from enemy attack.

These days the citadel has become a museum.

A stout electric trolley car takes you deep into the hillside for a powerful theatrical portrayal of the horrible battle of Verdun. The passages are cold and dark. The story is told through narration, film, sound effects and living, speaking holograms of military personnel. Theatrical sets are brought to life by dim illumination which fades in and out as you pass.

THE FORT OF DOUAUMONT

Construction began in 1885. It had the reputation of being the strongest fort in Europe. It has two subterranean levels protected by a reinforced concrete roof twelve metres thick.

The fort fell to the Germans a few days after the Verdun offensive began on 21st February 1916.

Most of the French garrison had gone to the lower levels to escape the constant German shelling with large calibre guns and howitzers.

A German squad of about ten men approached and entered the fort without a single shot being fired. It proved a useful shelter and first aid station for German troops.
It was recaptured some eight months later.

THE OSSUARY OF DOUAUMONT

Moslem graves at Verdun. In the background is the central tower of the ossuary (bone house).

Ossuary – a receptacle of bones of the dead; a charnel-house in which bodies or bones are piled.

The ossuary was built at one of the most fought over locations of the battle of Verdun. The long building houses the shattered bones of an estimated 130,000 unidentified French and German soldiers which were picked up from the surrounding battlefields.

The huge quantity of bones and bone fragments fills alcoves within the building and can be seen through small windows.

Outside, in the huge cemetery, 15,000 soldiers are buried under the fields of crosses. Many of them are marked simply *"Inconnu"* (Unknown).

The ossuary has a central tower, forty-six metres high which provides a panoramic view over the battlefields. The tower contains a death-bell and a lantern which shines at night over the battlefields. The tower represents a sword buried deep in the earth but the crosspiece of the hilt is only made at night by beams from the lantern. The shape of the tower is also reminiscent of a shell.
These days pine trees cover almost the entire battlefield – only they will grow in the soil still poisoned by chemical warfare agents.
Much of the landscape around Verdun bears the scars of constant heavy bombardment with shells, closely pockmarked with shell craters which have become weathered and grassed and softened by time.

WAR WOUNDS

Wounds can be very deep and memories very long in Verdun.

Even now, in the first decade of the twenty-first century, that terrible battle manages to cast its long dark shadow and there people alive in the town who have a direct to it.

There are people still alive who were made orphans by the battle of Verdun, people whose families were destroyed. It's impossible to imagine the effect such destruction could have on you for the rest of your life.

I was in Leclerc's supermarket one day and didn't realise I had to weigh all my items of fruit and veg before presenting them at the checkout. The checkout girl decided the quickest way to deal with this errant customer was to desert her post and weigh every item and stick on price labels herself.

There was a very old lady behind me in the queue. *"Pardon Madame, je suis desolé"* (Forgive me, madam, I'm very sorry) I said with all the sincerity and French pronunciation I could muster, but that woman gave me a look of pure hatred before she turned her head away. I'm pretty sure that was a look she reserved for someone she thought to be German.

POSH CAMPERS

I go to the posh end of the campsite where the static caravans have balconies. I'm in search of a washbasin with a plug.

I'm wearing black trousers with very sturdy, two-inch wide red braces (designed for supporting heavy leather motorcycle jeans).

One of the posh caravans has four people sitting at a table on their terrace eating a meal and drinking wine.

As I pass I hear a woman whisper *"Est-il français?"* (There is much speculation on this campsite as to the nationality of other campers - whether they are French, English or German). Her female friend replies, *"Je ne sais pas, mais ses bretelles sont très jolies!"* ("I don't know but his braces are very attractive!"

THE CAMPSITE AT NIGHT

Tonight there are voices all over the campsite. Moving round like mischievous spirits. Laughing, growling, mocking. It could be children making mischief but I imagine them to be the unhappy souls of men cut down in battle come to taunt those lucky enough to be still alive.

You can imagine all kinds of things when there is only thin fabric between you and the night air and there are strange noises about. I'm restless all night and unzip the door at dawn to see the grass is wet and there is a mist.

I get up and take some photographs of cobwebs hung with moisture drops.

BUCKFAST ABBEY, DEVON

October 25th 2009

My Honda Hornet 600 outside Buckfast Abbey.

Buckfast Abbey is on the edge of Dartmoor. I love this place and it's my third visit as a guest.

Saint Benedict told the monks they had to take in guests (in those days I imagine mostly waifs and strays) and be nice to them. They still do that to this day although these days quite a few of the guests are Catholic priests on retreat.

Me in the guest lounge.

You pay what you can afford although there is a suggested daily amount for full board.

Only men are allowed to stay in the monastery itself and eat (in silence) with the monks.

Buckfast Abbey was abandoned in 1539 as a result of the

dissolution of the monasteries instigated by spiteful Henry the Eighth when the Catholic church wouldn't allow him to divorce. Henry founded the Church of England at the same time.

The abbey buildings fell into disrepair and many blocks of stone were removed for local building projects.

Light from a stained glass window.

In 1882 a small community of mostly French monks re-founded the site.

The present buildings were constructed between 1907 and 1937 by the monks themselves – there were six of them, one with masonry experience. Scaffolding was made of wood and the abbey has photos of monks working on the buildings.

I was in the church twice today. First at two thirty when a male voice choir filled every crack and corner of that vast church with almost physical waves of sound. Then at nine PM I was there when the soft chants of Compline made their gentle magic to protect us all and chase away the demons of the night.

An icon I painted for the monks during one of my stays.

After Compline the monks are not allowed to speak until the following morning.

Today I chatted to Father D in the guest lounge. Here are some of the things he said.

"We've lost the significance of our symbols. A white wedding dress represents virginity and purity but I get weddings where the bride is in white and her three children are the bridesmaids and she's pregnant with the fourth.

"I once did a funeral where the deceased had been familiar with criminal activity. Three mourners arrived handcuffed to policemen. There was a police helicopter overhead and police in the bushes. One of the handcuffed mourners asked if he could be released from his handcuffs to throw some soil onto the coffin. His request wasn't granted. I didn't know the deceased and didn't say anything negative about him. I think I said something like 'and God is the final judge of our lives.'

"At Christmas I tell my young parishioners 'Christmas doesn't exist for Father D.' What I mean is I won't have anything to do with the dreadful commercial aspects. The tacky store displays in September and October for instance.

"People say, 'You must live a sheltered life as a priest, away from real life.' The reality is quite the opposite. I've been a priest for twenty-five years. You meet and interact with every imaginable kind of human being. You develop a sixth sense about people. Before they even speak you know quite a bit about them. A great deal of our knowledge about people comes from their body language. We unconsciously monitor it all the time. As a priest, your reading of body language becomes acute.

"I haven't worn a dog collar for about twenty years. It creates a distance between me and people. A distance I don't want. The only time I wear the full uniform is if I need to gain quick access to for example a hospital. I once had to visit a young parishioner in hospital. I avoided all the fuss and went straight to his bedside. 'Father D', he said, 'why are you wearing that?' He'd never seen me before in a dog collar."

I suggested that perhaps some priests like the uniform because of the status and advantages it gives them. He agreed it could become a kind of addiction.

I asked Father D if a priest looking like a priest affects the way people react.

"It certainly does. They see you as a stereotype and expect you to behave in certain ways. Often I've been with a group of people and someone has asked me what I do. I tell them I'm a Catholic priest. Immediately their attitude changes and they go into 'what should I do in front of a priest?' mode. That's when they start asking questions about religion and expect me to have all the answers to everything.

"One evening about five-thirty after a terrible day, I answered the door and found a male parishioner with some kind of a problem which he thought needed my immediate attention. My face must have shown the way I was feeling because he said, 'At least you could smile.' 'Why?', I asked him. 'If you'd just had a day like I've just had you wouldn't be smiling.' They think you shouldn't be subject to normal human behaviour even though you're a normal human."

Father D proceeded to tell me a joke.

"A man arrives in Heaven. God says, 'Whatever you do, don't go behind that wall.' 'Why not?' asks the man, to which God replies , 'Because that's where I keep all the Catholics and they think they're the only ones here.'"

I ask Father D if he ever considered becoming a monk.

"It's a calling", he says, "and besides which I'm so used to doing things my own way that I'd find the strict structure and being told what to do all the time difficult. It's just not me … but I love coming here for a break."

I'm at the side gate checking on my bike when a very elderly nun in a black habit arrives, stops by the gate and searches through her handbag. She has stunning blue eyes. I hold the gate open and ask her if she wants to come through.

"No, I'm just checking if I've got my house key."

"And have you?"

"Yes, it's here."

Do you think it's going to rain today?"

"I wouldn't like to prophesy."

"Probably wise."

"Yes. Goodbye."

"Goodbye."

I learn later that the woman is Dame Christine, the last surviving member of a French seventeenth century Benedictine order. When she dies, that's it. The order dies with her. She was married and when her husband died eighteen years ago she moved here and lived with two other nuns in a big house in the monastery grounds. Eventually the other two nuns moved away but Dame Christine chose to live in the house alone. I'm so glad I've met her.

A weir on the river Dart as it flows through Abbey grounds.

Detail of a window.

The refectory here is large and rectangular with long tables around three sides.

Cotoneaster on a wall outside the monastery.

At lunch time and evening meal time there is a biblical reading followed by a reading from a contemporary book (not necessarily a religious one). Just now *Sisters of Syria* is being read each day. There's some great humour in it.

At the far end of the refectory the Abbot (Father Abbot) sits in the centre of the table with Father Prior (I think that's what he's called) beside him. The seating is hierarchical with the two novices far removed from the Abbot.

These days the Buckfast order is only twelve strong.

The guests sit together but separate from the monks.

The Abbot sits under a painted Crucifixion.

The clinking of cutlery and crockery, footsteps on the tiled floor, a cough, a whisper. The silence is surprisingly noisy.

There has been a monastery on this site for nearly a thousand years.

One lunchtime I notice sunlight streaming in through a mullioned window and illuminating part of the white hair and the side of the face of an old monk.

The guest lounge.

Wednesday October 28th 2009

Today was very special. It was a feast day to celebrate the re-founding of the monastery by the mostly French monks in 1882.

Normally the mood in the refectory is ordered and solemn as the monks arrive after one o'clock prayers. Today the mood was joyous and playful. It was a Christmas mood. The monks were allowed to communicate with each other and the guests over the meal. Normally the loudest sounds are the clinking of cutlery and crockery but today the refectory was alive with chatter and laughter. The monks were transformed from cold, emotionless automatons to warm and vibrant human beings. The chain of silence was lifted and loving emotion rose from their hearts.

The food, as always, was fantastic. The main course was braised steak which fell apart. Also today there was wine.

It was a fantastic occasion and the afternoon prayer was dropped to make way for a holiday afternoon.

This afternoon I spoke for the first time to Father Sebastian who is eighty years old and has been here sixty-one years. It's difficult to comprehend that this very old gentleman started as a novice here when he was nineteen.

He is a fertile composer and musician. Many of his compositions have been published. He plays the organ for Mass every morning at eight o'clock and practices daily. He has two parishes to attend to.

A while ago he had an accident in the monastery car (the monks are not allowed to individually own things) when I think he backed into another car. The police prosecuted him for driving without due care and attention but he charmed the magistrate to the extent that he was let off.

BUCKFAST ABBEY, Devon, October 2010

There is no Compline tonight because of a Handl concert in the church. A busy day for the church - this afternoon there was a wedding.

Guest Master Brother Daniel joins me in the guest lounge after supper. I ask him how long he has been a monk here.

"Thirty-one years. I joined in 1979. I was a child the first time I saw the monastery. My father worked for a company that was involved in supplying stone for the rebuilding of the church."

(That began in 1907 and was completed in 1938).

"We came here for a family outing when I was eleven. As I looked around I thought it might be a good place to come when I was older.

I put the thought to the back of my mind, then when I left school I worked for Sainsbury's for about ten years.

I applied to come here when I was in my mid-twenties. At first I was interviewed by a senior monk. He asked me some questions, gave me some information and told me to go away and think about it for a while. This I did then I put in a formal application. I was interviewed by the Novice Master. One of the questions he asked me was, "Do you know what is meant by the married state?" I said I did. I'd already had one or two girlfriends and knew very well what he meant. I never felt I'd be much good at being married. I knew I'd have had problems coping and in the end I would have let my wife down.

The Novice Master asked me if I was a Catholic. He asked me the name of my priest and my doctor. He asked me to think about any mental problems there might be in the family because such things could surface in me as a result of the strenuous and isolated nature of monastic life.

I already knew this was what I wanted to do for the rest of my life. I had no doubts at all.

My father asked me how I would deal with 'manly passions'. My mother cried because she wanted grandchildren and didn't want me to go away. That was all thirty-one years ago now, in 1979.

In some ways it's not an easy life but it has many compensations. I worked with the bees for fifteen years. It was out in the open and fascinating work.

I worked in the kitchen for several years and I've been Guest Master for the past six.

I've enjoyed all the different jobs I've been given. I've tried to approach each one of them with the same eagerness and desire to serve. Benedict called it 'unhesitating obedience (with no grumbling in the heart)'. The first step towards humility. All tasks should be carried out with uncomplaining humility.

I miss being outdoors like I was when I worked with the bees - a Guest Master spends most of his time within the confines of the monastery buildings - but I love the work nonetheless.

I learnt today the true circumstances of Father Sebastian's car accident a year or two back.

Lovely, quirky old father Sebastian (who is a composer of some note) was out in a monastery car visiting his two parishes. He took the Ashburton turn-off but failed to see a coned-off truck on the slip road and drove into the back of it, turning the car over and writing it off. The cataracts in both eyes couldn't have helped with his hazard awareness.

Father Sebastian charmed his way into the magistrate's heart and escaped with a modest fine and a promise to get his eyes looked at.

The brethren were rather hoping his license would be taken from him but he escaped that indignity and he continues to drive to this day (but he has had his cataracts seen to and he sees a little better than before).

The small white toaster has recently been pressed into service because the big black one went wrong. This morning, however, there was also a problem with the white toaster.

I put in two slices of bread and pressed the lever. At that point Father Sebastian came over and took control.

"That won't work", he said, *"The bread is quite the wrong consistency for toasting and buckles inside, jamming the mechanism."*

Meals are meant to be eaten in silence but the rule is not hard and fast - if there's good reason then it's ok to talk.

"There's too much moisture in it. This is what you have to do."

I moved out of the way so he could get nearer the toaster. He delicately operated the lever again and again until the untoasted bread emerged a few millimetres at a time. Eventually he was able to lift the slices out. He put in two fresh pieces of bread, turned on the toasting timer but didn't lower the bread into the device. Just the lower part of the bread began to toast. After a short time he lifted out the bread, inverted it and put it back into the toaster and toasted the other end in the same way. This gave the bread enough stiffness to toast properly without jamming the mechanism. When the toast was ready, Father Sebastian operated the lever and triumphantly withdrew the intact and perfectly toasted slices of bread.

"You're an expert", I said, *"In fact you're the Toast Master!"*

He went back to his seat chuckling with delight at his triumphant performance.

TRAVELLER'S TIP - Take a plastic food box for small things (the things you are most likely to lose). It keeps them together and makes the room tidier. You'll always know where things are.

Text messages, GUARDA, Portugal, May 2012

Hello Frank. Not quite cold enough for snow. Just saw a large man dragging a small dog and back half of dog disappeared down a large drain hole in the kerb. He yanked the dog out and both man and dog carried on as though nothing had happened.

I managed to sink ham, cheese, apricots, a buttered roll and coffee for breakfast. I think the octopus tentacles I eat last night pulled it all down. Change of plan - will head for Porto on the coast today. I believe it's where the name port comes from. Should be warmer at sea level.

I'm stopped by the roadside for mango nectar and photos and wouldn't be at all surprised to see a Roman legion marching down the road. All around vineyards, olive groves, men working in the fields, skin almost black with sun, and in the villages, mosaic pavements and beautiful blue and white tiled panels on building site hoardings.

Text messages, PORTO, Portugal, May 2012

Hi Frank. Crossed the River Douro on my way here - it must have been over a hundred yards wide. Porto is at its mouth. Will establish if there's a connection between Porto and port later. Big city. Hope to find a motorcycle mechanic to adjust headlamps for right-hand driving. Might drink a drop of port as well.

It seems port wine is indeed named after Porto, the exporting port. (o porto means the port in Portuguese). Grapes grown inland over a big area and the wine is made inland. Interesting place. Huge city but the historical bit manageable. Big Sandemann figure overlooks the magnificent, wide River Douro. Pension adequate - single room with breakfast and garage space, €30.

Big May Day fiesta today, Frank. Boozing in street, marching bands, national holiday. It's great.

Eating my breakfast of ham and cheese. I think I'm one of very few guests in this hotel. It's a bit sinister at night on the street with cops on corners and wasted druggies wanting to mug you. Last night I was out looking for food and a thin, dark guy was watching me and following. He kept dodging down little side streets and appearing in front of me. It was scary. He'd stand on a corner and watch me approach him. In the end I put my hand in my back pocket, hoping he'd think I had a knife. As I approached him I pulled out my closed fist and slowly brought it round to my front. That did the trick - he faded away after that. Those demon thieves must be lying around in an opiate haze.

It's a clear, blue sky today, Frank. Too hot to go out. Resting on bed.

The manager of the Hotel Porto Rico where I'm staying has told me if I stay two weeks or more he'll charge €25 a day instead of €30. That's worth considering. Had a good laugh with Claudia the chambermaid today. She's a delightful young woman.

Just wandered into a military establishment by mistake, looking for a bridge. Young soldier on guard didn't know quite what to do so he saluted me. I would have returned the compliment but saluting's not in my repertoire of body movements.

Black suits, capes and hats are the order of the day as many hundreds of university students take over the city and walk around in large packs, boozing and loudly singing adapted traditional Portuguese songs. Fantastic.

Discovered a sort of council run Citizen's Advice Bureau today. Free internet access one hour a day.

Bought a blue baseball cap yesterday for €5. Drunk half a bottle of wine last night and left the hat on a café chair. It was gone today so I bought another hat (another €5). Now I have a camouflage hat and camouflage flip flops. Must learn how to salute.

Very hot. The graduate celebrations continue. Stumbled upon a Catholic service in a beautiful church. I'm doing the slow Sunday Portuguese walk.

Red wine pretty thin and bit sour (but was cheap). The port is rich, sweet, thick, luscious and potent but my favourite is the local white Douro - gentle and laid back - walks slowly, like the Portuguese. Just had half a bottle.

Think I'll stay the whole fifteen days here … I must really want that 20% discount!

Went out at dawn. Been photographing bridges, flowers, colourful washing - have to be discrete with the latter - can almost hear them thinking, *"Why do these people need photographs of our underwear?"* Fair point. I wouldn't like to find some Portuguese dude in the garden taking photos of my pants.

Had grilled mackerel, potatoes, rice, salad, bread and pint of beer earlier - £7. I shall come back here.

Gave my old shirt to a guy who lives in a cubby hole down the road - just bought a deep purple one to replace it.

Bought the *Times* today.

Ambulances don't just make the usual noise here - they bark as well.

University students now roaming the streets in colour-coordinated groups, the colour according to their faculty. I think even the professors are at it (or they're very old students). It's a bit Gormenghast. Matching t-shirt, top hat and cane. Orange, yellow, purple, pink, pale blue, copper to name a few colours. I've learned it's a very old tradition. The students now have been partying for five days.

Have found a peaceful library in a beautiful park with peacocks and the *Guardian* newspaper.

The students were noisily out in force till the early hours last night. Will it never end?

Went to Oceano Atlantico this afternoon, a few miles north of Porto. Big, surfing breakers, wide, sandy beaches and warm sea (so someone told me).

I left the ignition keys in my bike by mistake. A man saw them, put them in the ignition and stood guard till I got back. What a hero! … but a reluctant one because he walked off before I had a chance to thank him properly and give a bit of money for a drink.

Eat pork, rice, potatoes and pig's blood and finished with a chocolate éclair and couldn't resist a chocolate ice cream on the way back to the hotel for a nap.

Library this morning. A calm oasis. Weather cooler, some cloud.

Just went in a chemist that also sells wine and cat food.

Much coughing and spitting in the streets, especially from the women.

Wild boar omelette, salad, chips, bread and beer.

Rode the trams this afternoon.

On a train for Lamega, a mountain retreat. The tiled sanctuary and strange medieval tower were fiercely fought over by Moors and Christians (the Christians won eventually).

Accosted by a very well-dressed beggar. She wore a tweed suit and her hair was well-cut. Her glasses looked expensive. I didn't give her anything. She should have been offering me money.

Sunny spells. Coolish. Lots of folk in the library today.

Had double cheeseburger, chips, coke, M&M's MacFlurry and a milky coffee in MacDonald's last night. Traditional Portuguese fayre.

Waiting for mushroom omelette with fruit in it and salad.

Library this morning and photography museum and gallery in the old courthouse and remand prison. Historical exhibition of Porto street life in black and white photos. Excellent. Hundreds of mysterious holes in the granite walls, some of them three or four inches diameter. I speculated with the staff how they might have got there and we reckoned the prisoners somehow gouged them. It would have given them an interest!

My omelette has arrived with cucumber, tomato, pineapple and peaches.

Soapbag tragedy! Bottle of shower gel leaked into my rucksack and now the soapbag and its contents, a jumper, my map book, waterproof gloves and rucksack are all soaked. I washed them but it resulted in endless white froth and bubbles. Hairdryer got it sorted in the end. Memo to self - make sure all tops are on tight.

TRAVELLER'S TIP - Do your packing slowly. Start well in advance and gradually make a pile of what you think you'll need. As you move around your home, add things to the pile, then when you want to pack in earnest, get out your list and collect what you've missed.

PORTO, Portugal, May 2012

THE CHURCH OF BONES

São Francisco Church, Largo de São Francisco

The church has an incredible interior. There is a rather theatrical gilded wooden carving which must be about fifteen feet high. It represents a tree with a figure, presumably Jesus, lounging at its base. He supports the tree on his thigh and the roots trail all around. In the tree are the twelve disciples with Mary in an alcove. The carving is fully three-dimensional, very detailed and has huge presence.

A leaflet in the church explains that, until the 1860's, the Portuguese buried their dead in and around churches, but the public health authorities of the time decided the practice was in all probability not healthy and banned rotting corpses from inside church buildings. The dry bones of São Francisco church were gathered up and scattered over the floor of the big vault beneath the church. You can peer through gratings to see the bone-covered floor.

TRAVELLER'S TIP - Keep old packing lists - you'll always need more or less the same things so it's pointless making a new list every time you go away.

You might want to keep lists for summer and winter, for UK travel and for travel abroad. Keeping old lists will save you lots of time.

COLOURFUL BEGGAR WOMEN

I'm sitting outside a café in Batalha Square drinking coffee. A woman of perhaps sixty-five approaches. She is almost pear-shaped and wears a colourful headscarf and skirt. With her is a girl of maybe sixteen, similarly dressed. Probably her granddaughter. This is a lesson in begging for the girl.

The older woman surveys the tourists eating and drinking at the café tables, points to one and watches from a distance as the girl approaches a young black guy eating on his own. You can see he's a very relaxed, benevolent sort of guy - an ideal target.

A church in Porto.

The girl mimes to the man that she needs a drink. An angry waiter approaches and tells the girl to go away, but she stands her

Typical Portuguese shop, Porto.

San Bento station, Porto.

ground. The black guy mimes to the waiter, *"Oh, I'll get her a drink. Give her what she wants."* The waiter reluctantly goes into the café and comes out with a small bottle of an orange drink. The girl tells him it's not what she ordered! Having got this far she's not going to be palmed off with something she doesn't want. The increasingly angry waiter disappears into the café again and this time emerges with a can of Coke. This is what she wants.

The girl holds up the tin in triumph, as if to say, *"Grandma, haven't I done well?"*

She rejoins her grandmother who puts the tin in her swag bag and the two go in search of their next benefactor.

A skilful display of observation, psychology and nerve to divert a bit of tourist revenue their way. Who says beggars can't be choosers?

TRAVELLER'S TIP - Whenever you go away it's a good idea to take a list of important phone numbers with you. For example, what number to ring if your credit or debit card is declined, lost or stolen. You also might need your emergency vehicle breakdown number and your vehicle insurance emergency number.

I always make a note of my motorcycle key tag number so that if I did lose the ignition key (and the spare!) it would be a whole lot easier to get a replacement.

It's also a good idea to take a list of any computer passwords you might need - to enable you to access your bank account for instance.

THE GUAGE MAN

Some of the small shops here are unbelievably specialised. If you want to shop for any kind of second-hand gauge for example then there's a little shop down near the Porto waterfront that should be able to fulfill your needs. The window display and glass cabinets inside are stuffed full of gauges of every imaginable description - air pressure gauges; clock gauges to take tiny measurements; big, solid German gauges; water flow rate gauges; gauges that measure things I've never heard of; barometers; compasses; mechanical timers … but no clocks to tell the time.

At the back of the little shop is a doorway into a dimly lit room. There's a kind of wire mesh window but it isn't possible to see through it into the back room although I have a feeling I'm being watched from the other side of the mesh window. I can hear quiet radio music coming from the back room.

The shop surely has to be a manifestation of one man's obsession with gauges of all kinds, and judging by the quantity of them in the shop it has to be a long-held obsession indeed.

I imagine him spending his days in the room behind the shop taking apart, repairing, servicing and re-assembling his gauges to the gentle sound of Portuguese popular music.

I suddenly remember my own gauge - an excellent quality motorcycle tyre pressure gauge which I always carry with me on my adventures.

I resolve to bring it to the shop to show the man behind the mesh screen. Perhaps he'll get excited and offer me lots of money for it. In any case I'd love to take a photo of him standing by his wares.

I turn up later with my air pressure gauge in my pocket. The gauge man is standing in his shop doorway checking out a pair of binoculars by looking through them down the street.

When he's finished he greets me and I show him my gauge. He takes it, taps it, examines it, turns it over in his hand then launches into what I imagine to be an expert analysis, in rapid Portuguese. I protest that I don't understand but it makes no difference - he's going to tell me about it anyway in a language I don't understand. I nod and make noises of agreement every so often.

Eventually he finishes his analysis and hands the gauge back to me.

He invites me into his shop and takes an old barometer off the wall, opens the back and shows me the almost empty long, curved mercury tube. He goes into his workshop and emerges with two plastic 35mm film canisters and a large plastic pot, each half full of

Fernando Alves, the gauge man of Porto.

mercury. He invites me to pick them up and I'm amazed at how heavy they are - each film canister weighs perhaps a pound. He plunges a finger into the liquid metal in one of the film canisters and withdraws it completely clean. He then demonstrates through mime how he will replenish the glass tube with mercury and repair the delicate wheel and thread mechanism which moves in response to changes in atmospheric pressure and predicts how the weather is likely to change.

I'm genuinely interested in what he's showing me and he picks up on that because he enthusiastically invites me into the inner sanctum of his working life - his little workshop at the back of the shop.

It's a magical place lit only by a workshop lamp.

There's a small workbench with a little metal working lathe (maybe eighteen inches long) on which he must make parts to repair the precision instruments which are his stock in trade.

The workbench is strewn with beautiful tools - a tiny white penknife, the handle of which is inlaid with a lovely azure blue design; miniature pliers; small screwdrivers; tweezers; punches and hammers. I can see that all the tools are of fine quality. Beside the lathe is a small vice.

Over the bench is a shelf of spares and above that, another shelf on which is a row of jobs waiting to be done, each with a neat ticket attached showing the customer's name, estimate for the job and the date it should be ready for collection.

The music I heard earlier is coming from a CD player at the end of the bench, not from a radio as I thought.

The gauge man picks up an instrument and holds it lovingly and respectfully in the palm of his hand. The gauge has a series of holes around the metal side of the casing and I see the face is calibrated in percentages. The needle points to the upper sixties. The gauge man gently blows into a couple of holes and within a few seconds the needle rises a few percentage points. I think it must be a gauge for measuring the amount of humidity in the air and the moisture in his breath is causing the mechanism inside to react. There is a look of childish delight at the wondrous workings of the instrument.

I turn towards the shop and see that from the darkened workroom you can see quite clearly through the partly etched glass panel to the street beyond.

I indicate that I must go. He warmly shakes my hand and gives me

Portuguese tiles.

his business card. His name is Fernando Alves and the card lists some of the instruments he deals with - manometers, thermometers, barometers, altimeters, binoculars, microscopes and more.

I indicate that I'd like to take his photograph and we go back into the shop and he stands in front of an array of instruments for me. I make a mental note to send him a copy of the photograph.

TRAVELLER'S TIP - If you hang around office buildings at lunchtime and look out for hungry-looking people emerging with a purposeful step, they are probably heading for reasonably-priced food establishments. All you need do is follow them (but try not to get arrested for stalking).

Inside a church, Porto.

LANZAROTE AIRPORT NOVEMBER 2013

I'm on my way to Gran Canaria for a one night stopover then on to Dakar, the capital of Senegal for a few weeks winter sun. It's amazing how much better I can feel with an injection of hot winter sunshine.

My rucksack attracts a good deal of suspicion as it passes through the X-ray machine. It's because of the small fabric case containing my eight harmonicas, each of which has two metal covers covering the reeds.

I'm going to Senegal, once a centre of the slave trade, which is why I need my harmonicas. Those guys took their music from West Africa to the southern states of America and in their sadness starting playing the Blues. It's been my favourite form of music since I was fifteen and I've played blues harmonica since then (or blues harp as it's often called).

The X-ray monitor guy has probably never seen such an X-ray image before so it's fair enough that he gets me to unpack my rucksack so he can have a proper look.

He seems satisfied by what he finds and I repack my rucksack and heave it onto my back. Just as I'm about to leave the security area the monitor guy tells me to wait. He calls a uniformed woman over and whispers something to her. She comes up to me. *"You have harmonicas?"* she says. I agree that I do. *"I need to see your harmonicas,"* she says. She seems to be delighting in saying the word *harmonicas* which I imagine has only just entered her English vocabulary.

I'm very aware that my flight is due to leave in a few minutes but it's pointless arguing with these people.

Once again I unpack my rucksack. She's happy that the harmonicas are not explosive devices and I begin to repack. She sees my tube of factor 30 sunscreen which I bought the other day for £5. She wags her finger. *"Not allowed"*, she says. *"One hundred millilitres only."*

I'm getting very irritated. Is she deliberately trying to make me miss my plane? She indicates that I should dump it in the rubbish bin. I bet they do well out of all the thrown away stuff. My turn to be a bit awkward. I remember I have a small plastic bottle. I find it but it's full of talc. I shake it out into the bin, deliberately making a bit of a mess. The talc goes all over the top of the bin and on the floor. I decant a small amount of sunscreen into the bottle. She's satisfied (if a little irritated) and walks away.

I run down to the departure gate but it's too late; the plane is taxiing towards the runway.

I go back to the security people and tell them my flight has departed. They don't care, of course they don't.

The guy who spotted the harmonicas tells me I will have to buy another ticket.

"But it's your fault!", I inform him, but he just looks at me with the smugness of someone who knows they are undeniably in the right. He shrugs just to make absolutely sure I know his position.

The same woman walks me over to the ticket desk. I'm making a bit of a scene now and people are looking at me.

"For God's sake!" I say loudly, *"It's your fault. Why should I have to buy another ticket?*

The girl is very embarrassed. Good. She leaves me as we approach the airline ticket desk.

I say (as politely as I'm able to in the circumstances) to the girl on the desk, *"I was here on time but the security people just examined my bag for half an hour and I've missed my flight."* (Half an hour is an exaggeration but I've thrown caution to the wind and I'm quite beginning to enjoy myself).

She takes my boarding pass and without a word issues me a receipt for another ticket.

"Do I have to pay for this?" I ask. *"No"*, she says and smiles. A bit of sanity at last.

I get my new boarding pass and go through the whole procedure again. This time though they don't impede me and they both look slightly embarrassed. As I pass the woman and show her my boarding pass I wave the ticket receipt at her and say, *"Zero Euros!"* Just so she knows I won that battle. *"Sorry"*, she whispers.

I only have to wait twenty minutes or so before boarding the next plane to Gran Canaria. It's a rather lovely twin-engined petrol plane and when I see the beautiful red leather upholstery inside, my encounter with the security people is all but forgotten.

TRAVELLER'S TIP - Best not to take too many light coloured clothes - they show the dirt easily and need washing more frequently.

WEDNESDAY 4TH DECEMBER 2013

DAKAR, SENEGAL

I was looking for pegs in the local supermarket yesterday so I could hang out some washing on the wonderful sunroof here in the apartment block (or residential hotel as the owner prefers to call it) where I'm staying. I guess this place wouldn't even make one star but I love it all the same. The young guy who owns and runs it is called Cheikhna (pronounced Sheck-na with the first syllable accented) and he must be one of the most helpful people on the planet. When I first arrived here he padded with me through the sandy streets to the supermarket and gave me a tour of all the aisles.

In the supermarket I asked one of the young girls in my rudimentary French the whereabouts of the pegs. Her English was about the same standard as my French but we managed a pretty good conversation nonetheless. I'm getting good at changing from one language to the other mid-sentence if I can't think of or don't know a word or phrase. She was the same and we had a delightful bi-lingual conversation about pegs.

I must learn a few Wolof words - Wolof was the language spoken before the French arrived and imparted their language to the whole of North-west Africa, then I can drop those into conversations and impress the locals with my multi-lingual sentences.

The beach at Dakar.

It turned out they didn't sell pegs and the girl took me outside the store and pointed to a little shop where she thought I might be able to get them (as it happens they didn't sell them either and I had to be creative in hanging out my washing so it didn't blow off the line and end up five storeys below).

When we got back in the store she wrote down her mobile phone number on an old receipt and told me if I got into difficulties on any shopping expedition to dial the number and hand the phone to the shopkeeper and between them they should be able to sort it out.

In a similar vein, Cheikhna gave me his mobile number and said if I needed his help in any way to give him a ring.

Twice yesterday I needed his help when I got lost. The streets in this grown-up shanty suburb of Yoff all have the same name and a very similar appearance. Every road is called Rue Yoff and has a number. Many of the buildings look very similar. When I go to the supermarket I turn right at the end of Rue Yoff 367 into Rue Yoff 100, then left at the end of that road into the road (Rue Yoff but can't remember the number) which has the City Dia supermarket in

Tuna (I think) and fishing boats.

it.

These little local roads really do look similar to each other - even visiting Senegalese get confused, I've noticed.

The slightly more major thoroughfares have a good deal of tarmac

The sun roof at my apartment block.

exposed by the passage of horses, carts, scooters, buses, pedestrians and taxis (hundreds of them everywhere - clapped out yellow Peugeots, most of them with broken windscreens and giving off huge clouds of smoke - the air in central Dakar is hazy with it and must be pretty bad for the lungs if you live here (or even if you don't - I've certainly noticed it).

Off the main thoroughfares the hundreds of little side roads are all inches deep in sand with the tarmac (I'm assuming there's tarmac under there somewhere) not having seen the light of day for a long time I would think. I guess these little roads are coated with sand that's blown in from the Sahara which is pretty close to Senegal.

Anyway ... getting lost yesterday ... twice I apprehended a stranger and, in my very imperfect French, asked them to help me find my way home. These guys are amazing - they really go out of their way to help you if you're in any kind of trouble - even to the extent of walking you back to your hotel and seeing you safely inside. That happened once yesterday, after the guy had a long conversation with Cheikhna (pronounced Shek-na with a guttural k - an Arab name, he said it means a lucky charm or talisman) on my phone, explaining the location of the hotel (I can imagine the conversation went something like, *"Turn right into Rue Yoff, then at the end turn left into Rue Yoff then left again into Rue Yoff and you're there."* He got me back safely and Cheikhna was waiting at the door for me.

The other time (again after a long mobile phone conversation) Cheikhna came out to get me.

These guys are great.

The women you pass on the street are very friendly too - the great majority of Senegalese women are tall, slim and beautiful. They dress up in their brightly-coloured finery even to go to the supermarket and on Fridays their stunning, shimmering clothing rustles as they pass in a cloud of seductive perfume and tinkling jewellery. They really make themselves desirable to men (and I'm sure there's a good deal of competition going on between women too). They are extremely well-practiced in the secret female art of seduction handed down from woman to woman through the centuries.

If there's a woman walking towards you in the street (particularly a street in a poor area it seems) and you divert your eyes from her until you are just about to pass, it's guaranteed that when you look up, for a split second her stunning eyes seem to look right into your soul, then she looks away as if satisfied that her beauty has been given due respect. It's the whiteness of her eyes surrounded by her very black skin which surprises and delights - it's a very powerful (and quite erotic) experience to have a truly beautiful woman look directly into your eyes. If you say *"Bonjour"* she will happily reply and ask you how you are as you pass. Most of the men will too, but one or two have looked the other way, I'm not sure why. I have only seen a couple of women (out of the thousands I must have seen in Dakar) wearing the female Moslem head dress in public. This area of Dakar (Yoff) is very devout (the hotel has I think four small mosques within a radius of perhaps a hundred metres), but for some reason the women do not find it necessary to cover themselves in public … I think they must be very proud (and rightfully so) of their extreme beauty and want it to be on show. I'm glad they do.

On the beach two teenage girls in beautiful clothing were happy for me to take their photo (in fact they did a sinuous little dance for me), but when I asked the girl in the supermarket if I could take a picture of her and her male colleague - both wearing Christmas hats - she indicated that it was ok for me to photograph the young man, but not her. Maybe it's a personal preference thing, I'm not sure. I'll have to ask at the British Embassy later (along with all the other questions I have for them, including *"Why do some men look away when I greet them?"*)

I've seen a couple of middle-aged men (probably English - they both looked it) in the local supermarket, each with beautiful young Senegalese women maybe half their age. One guy was as red as a lobster with sunburn and I felt a bit sorry for him being dragged around the supermarket by his partner (who was rather obviously in charge). The family ties here are very close and very strong. Often there is a sizeable extended family living within a couple of streets of each other and I couldn't help wondering if these guys knew what they were letting themselves in for when they first formed a partnership with their women. A man from the West is seen as a good catch (for the whole poverty-stricken extended family) and I think it's fair to say that a fair bit of money is likely to be diverted from the man's bank account to members of the woman's extended family, in the same way as happens with young Thai and other Asian brides. This always makes me feel a bit uneasy, but I guess if you make your bed (literally) with a young Asian or African bride then you must be prepared to lie in it.

I met a young woman from Kuala Lumpur in England who had married an Englishman just in order to obtain a visa so she could live and work in England and send money back to her family (she was living in rather seedy and sad rented digs so it wasn't for her own benefit). She told me she returned home every year to visit her family.

Something a bit similar you get here (and I would think in other African countries) are middle-aged European women (particularly from the Netherlands around here, or so I've been told by a local male) who come to Senegal with the express intention of finding a young, fit African male to have an affair (or perhaps more than one). The young Senegalese men are incredibly physical - you see them running and playing football on the beach, doing press-ups, swimming, working all day in the hot sun on building projects - so I can understand the attraction for ladies approaching a certain age, let's say, but still it makes me feel uncomfortable - it seems to me as though the young men are being bought for sexual pleasure by relatively wealthy Western women … but again I suppose if everybody's happy then there's no harm done. Makes me feel uneasy nonetheless in the same way as do the older men with the young women. I imagine the women probably supply families of the young men with money but I'm not sure if that's the case or not.

TRAVELLER'S TIP - Do your packing slowly. Start well in advance and gradually make a pile of what you think you'll need. As you move around your home, add things to the pile, then when you want to pack in earnest, get out your list and collect what you've missed.

THURSDAY 12TH DECEMBER 2013

SENEGALESE CHRISTMAS

Christmas marketing is in full swing in the Citydia supermarket (which is less than a ten minute trudge through sandy streets for me).

A week ago it was the solitary line of chocolate Santas … now there's a Christmas tree with baubles and tinsel just inside the entrance and a couple of temporary tables with gold and silver coloured paper plates, dishes, cups and a selection of plastic cutlery. That seems to be about the extent of the Christmas effort although the other day I saw a couple of street traders walking around draped in Christmas decorations and carrying artificial trees. It seemed to me so incongruous to be selling Christmas trees and decorations in the hot sun.

Dakar (and possibly the rest of Senegal too, I'm not sure) is only two percent Christian so it's not surprising that the Christmas thing isn't done here on a big scale. Christians and Moslems respect each other's faith hugely here - Fridays and Sundays are both treated as holy days by each religion. Sunday feels to me very much like an old-style English Sunday - peaceful and quiet with both Christians and Moslems respecting it as a day of rest (of course it means there are two days of rest each week with a day of work in between - I guess that suits all parties).

Christmas at the City Dia supermarket, Dakar.

THE TAILOR
Just round the corner from where I'm staying in a narrow, sandy road there's a little tailor's shop. The guy who runs it is tall, gaunt,

dark coffee brown rather than black and probably in his early thirties. He seems very industrious and never seems to be short of work. I call in there one day and like the guy straight away - he has an air of honesty and integrity about him. Best of all he seems to understand my efforts at French better than most (some people don't even grasp that I'm trying to talk to them in French - I think they're expecting not to understand me and so they don't.)

The tailor and I come to an agreement that if I supply the cotton he'll make me a shirt and a pair of loose trousers for seven thousand francs (just less than ten pounds). I write in my notebook that I need one and a half metres for a shirt and two metres for a pair of trousers, but when I turn up the next day with one and a half metres of pale blue cotton he tells me I've got it wrong and I need two metres for a shirt and what's more, this material is no good at all for a pair of trousers because it's too transparent - I can see what he means when he holds it up to the sun and I can clearly see his fingers through the fabric.

My next attempt at cotton shopping is more successful - I turn up with two metres of pale pink cotton which he agrees to use for a shirt.

My third attempt results in a couple of metres of black cotton which he deems unsuitable for trousers but ok for a shirt.

So far, two shirts and no trousers. I'm determined to supply him with exactly what he needs and I enlist the help of a young local guy called Sidi (pronounced CD) whom I met at the hotel and who speaks fantastic English and seems to understand fabrics. He agrees to accompany me in a taxi to the Grand Yoff market to find what I need. We find a stall with a huge collection of materials and I choose a good quality, non-transparent cotton printed with a small black and white design. The girl stallholder won't cut the piece and I have to buy the whole six metres.

We turn up at the tailor's and he agrees it is highly suitable for trousers and another shirt. He agrees to have the three shirts and one pair of trousers ready for the following Wednesday evening for a total cost of eighteen thousand francs (about twenty-four pounds).

A Senegalese taylor.

Wednesday evening arrives. I call in and he hasn't even made a start on them. I agree I'll call in the following Monday for them on my return from Saint Louis. I just hope he's not going to be hopelessly unreliable. It's not looking good so far but time will tell. Watch this space.

The tailor turned out to be unreliable in the extreme. The day before I left Dakar he was absent from his shop but my little pile of fabrics was in the same place, unmoved and untouched. There was no point in me taking my fabric away so I left it there. It still peeves me a little that I went to all that trouble in finding exactly what he specified and then he made no effort at all to turn my cotton into garments. Oh well, I'll get over it and no doubt some time in the future (if he gets round to it) somebody else will be walking round in clothes made from fabric I paid for.

TRAVELLER'S TIP - If you take a small container (say a small plastic bottle of clothes washing liquid), you'll be able to stay on top of your washing whether on campsites or in hotels or hostels. You can do your washing in a sink, basin or bath and devise some way of hanging it to dry - perhaps a twisted string line. Alternatives - hotel or hostel washing service, a launderette, or don't do any and stink like a polecat.

In an emergency any kind of cleaning substance (shower gel, shampoo, washing-up liquid, a bar of soap for example) could be used for cleaning clothes (although bleach, floor cleaner and other such substances not recommended).

SATURDAY 18TH APRIL 2015

KUALA LUMPUR, MALAYSIA

I arrived in Kuala Lumpur by courtesy of a Malaysia Airlines Airbus A380 800 airliner - to date (2015) the largest passenger jet ever made. I sat in seat 67A just behind the port wing so I could watch the ailerons, flaps and air brakes operating (since taking up flying lessons last year I've become interested in things like that.) I had four seats in a row to myself and was able to lie down and sleep for three or four hours - the first time I've ever been able to sleep on an aircraft.

Last year Malaysia Airlines was unfortunate enough to lose two of its commercial airliners. One, an Airbus A380 was shot down by a missile over Crimea (imagine being a passenger looking out the window and seeing a missile speeding towards you), the other, a Boeing 777, disappeared entirely without trace somewhere over the Pacific Ocean and presumably making an unscheduled landing at the bottom of the sea.

These losses happened within four months of each other and as a result Malaysia Airlines lost about half of its customers (people became too scared to fly with them) and as a result were losing 3.6 million pounds a day. Eventually the Malaysian government took them over. Such a shame because it's a great airline but losing two aircraft in such a short space of time will stay a long time in public memory. The two main meals were the best airline food I've ever had although the snack in between of various types of sweet biscuit was a little odd.

I got a great deal from *Trailfinders* - Heathrow to Kuala Lumpur, three nights in the beautiful five star Majestic Hotel, Kuala Lumpur to Brisbane and a night in a hotel there, then the same flights and stops on the return trip - all for £1,277. I imagine a single night in a five star London hotel could cost considerably more than that.

The Majestic Hotel is truly wonderful. We have a reading room, a cigar room, a drawing room and an orchid room. The Indian gentlemen who deal with all matters transport (including free coach travel to various parts of the city) wear a British colonial uniform of pith helmet, off-white shirt, shorts with a black belt, long socks and black shoes.

I wasn't at all sure how to approach the huge and largely unfamiliar selection of breakfast items so I just plunged in and took what I thought I'd like.

First course was thinly-sliced meat (not sure what) with soft, strong cheese and coffee. Second course was pieces of pork and beef with rice, lettuce, a savoury sauce and more coffee. For a third course I had beef bacon, chicken sausage, fried rice, baked beans and more coffee. I finished off with a cheese and mushroom omelette but was so full I could only eat half of it.

I was intending having a swim in the beautiful fourth floor open air pool directly after breakfast but postponed it for an hour or so in case I sank to the bottom. I've never forgotten the kid who drowned in our local pool when I was a child. The post mortem discovered that the huge breakfast of sausages and bacon he'd eaten just before swimming had made its reappearance in his throat while he was at the bottom of the diving pool and in his

The Orchid room, Majestic Hotel, Kuala Lumpur.

panic he'd somehow got his fingers jammed in the metal grate which drained the pool. By the time they reached him he was dead.

Talking of the dead, I was walking along by the river this afternoon and came across two Malaysian men solemnly discussing whether an old Indian gent lying on the path was dead or just sleeping. I stopped and gazed for a minute or so and I must admit he didn't appear to be breathing. He looked so comfortable and serene lying on his side with his head resting on his bag. He'd either fallen asleep like that or died like that. After a while the two men shrugged their shoulders and walked off. Shortly afterwards I did the same.

I learned today that Kuala Lumpur means 'muddy estuary'. and was built at the confluence of two rivers.

I live by a muddy estuary myself (the Thames Estuary).

THURSDAY 7TH MAY 2015

DARWIN, Northern Territory, Australia

Darwinians are obsessed with crocodiles. It seems every day in the *Northern Territory News* there is at least one croc story.

I went to an exhibition of *NT News* front pages. There must have been fifty or so of them, representing the sixty or so years since the newspaper's inception. Many of the banner headlines were mildly amusing (example; *They Stole My Dog When I Was On The Bog*), but the range of subjects was pretty narrow with crocodiles and women's anatomy featuring heavily. Maybe fifteen front page stories related to crocodiles eating local dogs. The crocs were then caught and sold to breeding farms where they are bred for their skin and food value.

My favourite front page photo was of a crocodile eating a shark.

The Northern Territory still has a lawlessness about it (it's always been a good hiding place for crooks with its thousands of kilometres of red dirt roads).

Until 2014 there was no speed limit at all on the out of town roads … now it's 130 kph (in all other parts of Australia the maximum is 110). Many Darwinians would like to revert to the old days of no speed limit.

MAY 2015, Pine Creek, Northern Territory, Australia
Pine Creek is about two hundred kilometres south of Darwin and owes its existence to the discovery of gold in the area. The gold prospectors have long gone and the little town has the feel of a place that's lost its purpose and is barely hanging on to save itself from returning to the wilderness it once was.

Pine Creek has more than its fair share of wiry old timers with long, straggly beards who are unhelpful and uninterested in you to the point of being rude. They'd rather you weren't there but they need your cash so they, begrudgingly it seems, sell you something from the shop or let you hire a motel room.

It's a very strange place indeed.

I went in the local museum and found it depressing and uncared for. The arrangement of historical artifacts seemed completely random and many of the exhibits were virtually at floor level so you couldn't even see them properly. There were cobwebs everywhere and all the exhibits were covered in a thick layer of dust. It felt like someone long ago had had the idea of a museum but then lost interest halfway through setting it up.

The whole town has an air of lethargy and depression about it. There was nothing there once, then there was a mad, spirited gold rush, now there's almost nothing there again. Whatever crazy, hopeful spirit arrived with the gold prospectors (largely Chinese) has long since departed.

FRIDAY MAY 8TH 2015

En route to Australia Zoo, Beerwah, Queensland, Australia

I ask a station worker if it would be safe to walk to the zoo on the highway.

STATION WORKER *"Oh mate, there's some big trucks use that highway."*

ME *"I wouldn't want to end my days being run over by one of those."*

STATION WORKER *"I can think of better ways."*

ME *"Probably better to be eaten by a croc."*
(Pause)

STATION WORKER (Smiling) *"You'd get more publicity that way, mate,"*

MAY 2015

Australia Zoo, Queensland, Australia
I saw the good and the bad today. The beautiful and the terrible.
On the bus to Beerwah (Steve Irwin's Australia Zoo is near there and I decided to wait for the bus rather than risk being run over by an Australian juggernaut) I sat behind a stocky, solid guy in his thirties I would think, whose shaven head revealed a disturbing tattoo on the back of his head. The tattoo consisted of two Nazi storm trooper SS lightning flashes, maybe an inch high, and to the

right of that the numbers 14/88. I know this relates to respect and admiration for Adolf Hitler and his ways. (I think the numbers stand for alphabet letters … so that would be AD/HH. I'm not quite sure how that relates to Hitler, but I'm pretty certain it does). I hate to think what sort of person the tattooed man might have been but I'm pretty sure he's someone I wouldn't want to know.

Then at the zoo I saw one of the most beautiful and moving things I've ever seen. I headed straight for the Asian part of the zoo where tigers are kept in a part they call Tiger Temple. There is exquisite Indian music playing and the two tigers I saw are kept in a big enclosure with tall, mature bamboo plants, a big pool and lots of room to play or hide away among the bamboo canes.

There are no bars, just glass separating them from the visitors.

I got there late in the day and for a while I was the only visitor watching them.

I saw two keepers in the compound and with them two tigers lay like big domestic cats, completely at ease. The two keepers stroked and patted them as they talked to each other.

It was such a magical, perfect moment I saw through the glass.

I spoke to one of the young women attendants w

She told me that the two tigers were young brothers and they had been separated from their mother soon after birth and each tiger had lived with one of the keepers who were now in the enclosure. They had been brought up with the keepers and their families rather like domestic cats.

One of the tigers had been born with an inherited eye disease which caused cataracts in each eye. They had operated, but unsuccessfully and that tiger was now completely blind.

Both tigers had learnt to trust their keepers entirely, which explains why they were completely at ease with them in the enclosure.

I watched them playing and moving around their enclosure for perhaps half an hour. The eyes of the blind one shone with white

Tiger with its beautiful camouflage.

Tiger playing with a barrel.

milkiness.

It was wonderful to see their relationship and how the blind one felt his way around with his paws and listened out for where his brother was and what he was doing. Sometimes the sighted one would be resting and the blind one would stumble into him and the sighted one would immediately engage him in a play fight as if to say, *"Yes, here I am. Let's have a game."* When they were playing like that it didn't matter that one was blind - it was two tigers playing confidently in their own space.

It was truly beautiful how the sighted tiger helped out and looked out for his blind brother.

Like domestic cats, either of those tigers could, I am sure, turn in an instant into the fearsome killers they are just beneath the skin.

Steve Irwin when he died (he was killed by a big sting ray which whipped round and stabbed him) left a fantastic legacy. He loved wild animals of all kinds and set up a beautiful big zoo dedicated to teaching us about the animals and helping to breed rare species.

A board somewhere near the tiger enclosure says that a few decades ago there were an estimated one hundred thousand tigers living free in Asia. Now there are thought to be about five thousand.

To my mind the tiger is one of the most perfect of God's creations, with its fluid, graceful movement, pin-sharp instincts and stunning camouflage stripes. (It was really difficult to see them against the orange-yellow bamboo trunks with their vertical shadows.)

It would be an unspeakable tragedy if Man were to be responsible for the extinction of the tiger.

I'm so glad I visited Steve Irwin's zoo today and saw those beautiful creatures.

TRAVELLER'S TIP

Think light and small. No need to take a whole container of shower gel – take only what you need in a smaller plastic bottle. Sugar? Coffee? Tea bags? Dried milk? Decant what you need into smaller plastic or glass containers. Camping shops often sell small plastic containers

While you're there you can look round for other compacting ideas. For instance, you can buy highly absorbent towels (made from a synthetic textile a bit like chamois leather), which pack into their own small bags. A medium one packs up to about 20cm X 10cm X 2cm and it's truly amazing how much water they can hold.

Another thing you might consider is a pen torch about the size of a fat cigarette.

OCTOBER 2008

Hamburg, Germany

The famous Reeperbaum street in the red light area of Hamburg is a short train journey from where I'm staying and one night, like any good tourist, I get the train there to check it out. The Reeperbaum road itself is wide and feels very artificial to me – a well-lit tourist walk. I'm more attracted to the minor dark streets off the main drag so I turn away into one of the side roads then take a right into a street that's parallel to the Reeperbaum. It's dark and sinister here. I pass by three figures within a few feet. The first is a large, blonde woman in her forties I would think. She gives me an inviting smile which changes to a look of contempt as I pass her.

The next is a tall, slim black girl, maybe eighteen or nineteen years old. She looks at me coldly as I approach and pass her. The final figure is a dark-skinned man of about thirty, maybe an Arab. A minder or a pimp I guess. As I walk away from them they comment on me and laugh, but I don't understand what they say. I turn down a side street which leads back towards the main drag. As I walk, women hiss at me from the other side of the street to attract my attention, but I don't look at them. I fear they may have the power (or me the weakness) to make me cross the road to them and then I shall be swallowed into an attractive iniquity, robbed, beaten, murdered and never seen again.

I'm glad to get back onto the Reeperbaum itself. At least this busy tourist walk feels safe.

TRAVELLER'S TIP – If you need to buy something but don't know how to ask for it in the shop, do your ground work prior to shopping. Explain to someone who speaks your language what it is you want and get them to write down its name in the native language. You can then present the shop assistant with the piece of paper and they will know straight away what you require.

Sometimes you can draw a little picture of what you need and show that to the shop assistant. In Verdun I had great success in obtaining a universal sink plug by drawing a little diagram.

OCTOBER 2008

An Autobahn, Germany

I'm on my way from Hamburg to North Friesland and the real objective of this adventure – the artist Emil Nolde's house and gallery. He's long been my favourite artist and I have wanted to visit the Nolde Foundation at Seebüll which is on the Danish border very near the coast.

I do ridiculous speeds on the Autobahn and draw close to the maximum speed of my Kawasaki Z1000. Exhilarating and exciting and 140mph doesn't seem as fast as I think it should. I touch that for a second or two when a Porsche pulls aside to let me pass. The wind resistance is huge, so I get down as much as I can and lay almost flat along the tank. It's amazing how quickly you approach cars at that kind of speed, but most of them pull into the right-hand lane when they see a rapidly approaching motorcycle in their mirrors. I don't need to use my brakes; just throttling off slows me quickly.

I soon reach Seebüll, in its flat, reclaimed landscape (Büll means new land and many place names round here include the word – Klanxbüll, Niebüll and Dagebüll for instance).

Houses are built on little hills to protect them from high water if it ever breaches the defences.

A windy landscape of wide fields streaked with ploughed channels, water-filled.

I suddenly understand one of my favourite of Nolde's watercolours – big, heavy, purple-blue clouds underlit with red sundown light with paler red streaks in the fields. I see now this is setting sunlight reflected in the waterlogged field channels.

The Foundation offers accommodation for €65 a night (including breakfast). I decide to stay. I am the only guest in the huge farmhouse which was built in 1867 (the year of Nolde's birth), and was owned by Nolde until his death in 1956. One of the lovely sky-blue eyed ladies tells me his parents lived there. It has a thatched roof and one part of the building has a number of rooms for guests. I'm given Number 2 and it's a beautiful room facing south-west.

On the wall over the bed near the window is the very picture I mentioned and I see through the window that it may well have

Nolde's house where his parents lived and where I stayed.

been painted from this very room. It's advertising an exhibition in

Japan and the poster is very beautiful with its Japanese script in white.

A brooding Friesian sky. You can just see the lights of Nolde's house.

I can really feel Nolde's presence here, as though he's still very much interested in what goes on in his houses.

It was his wish that his house be used as a gallery for his pictures and the Foundation has done a fantastic job in displaying them. The top floor of the house is a beautiful gallery. Nolde liked a lot of pictures together, not just one surrounded by a lot of space and this is how they are displayed.

The exhibition changes regularly in order to show as many of his pictures as possible. He was a very productive artist.

Nolde is classed as one of the German Expressionist painters. His pictures (oils and watercolours) are powerhouses of brilliant, harmonious colour. Many of his paintings verge on the abstract. His watercolours (in which he used not just transparent watercolour paints, but also a lot of opaque body colour – gouache) are some of the most beautiful and powerful ever painted and often have a freedom and spontaneity which is lacking

A corner of the house with one of Nolde's images.

in some of his oil paintings. Later in life he transposed some of his freely painted watercolours into oil paintings but the results can feel laborious in comparison.

He kept pots of ready-diluted watercolour paints to hand so he could be spontaneous without wasting time mixing the paints.

I'm sure he felt most at home with watercolour. It's sometimes looked down upon by artists and critics as being the most insubstantial and lightweight of any painting medium but it is perhaps the most difficult medium of all and some would say requires more skill than any other medium. Oils and acrylics you can change and retune as much as you like. Watercolour has to be right first time. When painting a wet in wet watercolour (where wet paint is applied over wet paint) you are truly flying by the seat of your pants. The medium is unpredictable. Colours flow where they will, according to the tilt of the paper, the wetness of the previous layers and the laws of physics.

Nolde's watercolours are true works of genius.

I'm hungry and make for the restaurant which has only been open a couple of years. It serves as a training ground for people disadvantaged by deafness. They are trained in catering and table service.

The food here is top class and reasonably priced. I order shrimp soup which arrives beautifully presented with sprigs of herbs and a swirl of cream. It is delicious. I look up the word and write it down for the waitress. The word is "köstlich". She's delighted. In fact I have three waitresses – apart from me there is only a couple eating and all the trainees need some work. I get fantastic attention and service.

My baked potato arrives. It is resting in a huge bed of sour cream and is sehr köstlich.

I have a cup of green Darjeeling tea and leave feeling ready to explore.

This area is usually windy (from the west). The wind is strong and cold. The flatness of the reclaimed land would at first seem good for cycling, but you'd have to be cycling north with a tail wind. Any other direction and you'd be severely hampered by a powerful head or side wind.

The Friesian cattle (this is Friesland) seem especially content.

Skeins of ducks or geese in their large V formations fly inland. Maybe they are migrating.

I go to my room and through the window see the dark, bulbous clouds which feature in so many of Nolde's paintings, and of course this land is where he would have seen them from.

Nolde was born in a village called Nolde in Southern Denmark (just a few kilometres away). He changed his surname to that of the village of his birth.

Him and his first wife Ada (pronounced AH-der) searched long and hard for land on which to build. His house (which he designed himself) was built between 1927 and 1937. He purchased the farmhouse where I'm staying at the same time as the land.

He was at first very happy here and very productive. It was their summer house – winters were spent in Berlin where he could be in contact with the art world and exhibitions.

Hitler took exception to Nolde's art and banned him from painting even though Göebbels had his pictures in his home! Nolde of course continued to paint but not in oils in case the smell of turpentine gave him away to any visiting SS officers.

He produced many small watercolours on thin Japanese papers which he hid under the floor and they weren't discovered until many years after his death. I saw a wonderful exhibition of them in London many years ago. The paper was so delicate and absorbent that it was hard to tell which side of the paper had been painted.

The Foundation has done (and continues to do) a great job in displaying his works and I am sure Emil Nolde would be proud of them.

I stay two nights, and because I am the only guest, receive some special privileges – the lovely blue-eyed ladies dry my clothes and allow me to use the kitchen normally out of bounds to heat water for tea (I think they are afraid I will burn down the house with my spirit stove!)

HARWICH TO ESBJERG FERRY

Wednesday 8th October 2008.

I'm on board the MS (Motor Ship) Dana Sirena and my Kawasaki Z1000 is safe and sound somewhere near the bottom of the ship.

We left Harwich (Essex) at 5.45 PM and are due to dock at Esbjerg some time tomorrow afternoon.

It's a beautiful and massive ship – two hundred metres long with a gross tonnage of 25,000 tonnes.

In the past, ferry ships were kept afloat literally and financially by carrying cars and their passengers but cheap air travel more or less saw an end to that type of business and other cargo had to be found.

This ship is half containers and half trucks, cars and passengers. Mine is the only motor cycle.

Someone told me the Dana Sirena is a really special ship – the only one of its kind in this part of the world.

Our voyage is as smooth as silk, largely due to the use of stabilizers which greatly reduce the amount of roll. Ships roll from side to side and pitch up and down the waves like a big dipper fairground ride. Aircraft behave in a similar fashion.

The most comfortable place to be in a storm is as near as possible to the centre of the ship where pitching and rolling is at a minimum.

This is a very relaxing environment and I have a cabin with a sea view. That amused me when I was booking this voyage – when at sea what else can one see through a porthole except lots and lots of sea?

I'm in my cabin writing this and outside the porthole there's a tiny bird, wings beating furiously and looking in at me. It's keeping up with the ship which must be sailing at about thirty miles per hour. I'm not sure what that is in knots.

Other people have seen the bird and say it seems to live on the ship amongst the containers.

I wander round the ship and chat to a few people. One of them introduces himself by telling me he's a musician. He turns out to be a lovely man of I would think about thirty. He's on his way to visit Esbjerg for the eleventh time with his male friend who doesn't have a lot to say.

"I just love being on ships", he says. I'm with him all the way on that one.

"We're going to a big Lutheran church where I shall ask them if I can play their organ. I rarely get refused", he tells me.

I bet he's brilliant and I'd love to hear him play but he doesn't have any arrangements so it might be difficult. He's so gentle, innocent and fragile.

I learn from him that the building of Esbjerg began in 1862, which makes it the newest of Danish towns.

In one of the bars is a group of Danish kids of about fourteen or fifteen. They are with two male teachers. There are maybe twelve in all, quietly playing folk music on recorders. It's beautiful. They then sing *Streets of London* by Ralph McTell from song sheets. It's unexpected and lovely.

They are all so well-behaved and respectful towards others. Their parents and teachers must have taught them well.

They've been on a UK tour, visiting folk clubs I would imagine.

I continue my journey round the ship and make the acquaintance of a very sick man who is accompanied by a retired teacher of English from Oxford who has a Danish wife.

At first I think the retired teacher is a vicar but on closer inspection I see he just looks like a vicar and what I thought was a dog collar is a thin white polo neck over which he wears a black, buttonless tunic. (My spell checker wanted the tunic to be bottomless). He looks as though he's probably Indian, Pakistani or Bangla Deshi.

We talk of gas prices, the Economy and cancer treatment – his sick friend (who it turns out is a teacher of Law) is on his way to be treated in Denmark. He was refused a particular cancer treatment in the UK and will be able to get it in Denmark for free.

I hope things go well for him but he does look extremely ill.

I look at my little Danish dictionary and try to learn a few words and phrases. *Ja* is yes, *nej* is no, *hej* is an informal 'hello'. *Tak* is thank you. Perhaps the most useful phrase for me will be *Taler De engelsk?* Which means 'Do you speak English?' I anticipate most of the replies to that question to be more *ja* than *nej*. Another useful phrase might be *Jeg har gået vild*, which my dictionary tells me means 'I'm lost'.

THE ORESUND BRIDGE

This links Denmark and Sweden. It starts as a tunnel then the road rises out of the sea and becomes a bridge. The other end is so far away that sometimes it's no more than a misty mirage. Beautiful

TRAVELLER'S TIP

Bananas. Easy food but keep them above freezing – if the cells freeze they get damaged and on thawing they become liquid and the banana tastes unpleasant.

COPENHAGEN

I find a hotel and ask if there's somewhere secure I can keep my bike. The young male receptionist points to a courtyard and says it's fine to ride my bike through the foyer!

Copenhagen at night.

THE ESBJERG TO HARWICH FERRY

The ferry leaves at 6.30pm. I'm very tired and go straight to bed. When we reach the open sea the cabin shakes and twists and there are alarming bangs and noises as the ship battles through the waves. I am woken on numerous occasions by violent lurches and crashing noises from way below. I'm on deck 7 (of 10). I hope my motorbike's alright down there. I peer through the curtains and see the sea is very rough. Big foaming waves and huge curtains of spray. It must be very windy out there. Bed is the best place. There will be many passengers being sick and feeling very ill out there.

I sleep well, considering, and rise at about 6.45. The sea is calm and the dawn is just beginning. It opens into a beautiful sunny day.

The Esbjerg to Harwich ferry.

I sleep well, considering, and rise at about 6.45. The sea is calm and the dawn is just beginning. It opens into a beautiful sunny day.

TRAVELLER'S TIP – Take a small shortwave radio. It can be fascinating hearing VHF transmissions in other places. Shortwave can pick up stations all over the world. Signals bounce off the ionosphere. It can be comforting in a strange country to hear broadcasts in your own language. Long wave has a longish range. For instance I listened to BBC domestic transmissions in Hamburg.

SANTANDER TO PLYMOUTH FERRY

Half an hour or so out of Santander the Captain comes over the loudspeakers and warns of bad weather ahead in the Bay of Biscay. A north-westerly force seven gale and eight metre waves is his prediction. All outside decks are dangerous and he declares them to be out of bounds. He says walking round the ship will be hazardous and the safest place will be in your cabin.

I take his advice and lie on my bunk waiting for the excitement to begin.

Our ship, the Pont Aven, is the 45,000 tonne flagship of Brittany Ferries and has ten decks. The lower ones are huge garages for up to 650 vehicles of all kinds. There are 650 cabins and up to 2,400 passengers. I imagine the weight of all the vehicles must act as a kind of ballast to help stabilise this magnificent ship.

I've been on many voyages but this one takes the biscuit for fear and excitement.

Before long the motion and noises of the ship become alarming and at times almost violent. My cabin creaks and groans as the ship twists but the most alarming noise of all is the huge hollow metallic bang every minute or two from way down below. I'm not sure what it is but it's quite a scary sound and when it happens the whole ship shakes like it's been hit with a huge hammer.

If we're going to get shipwrecked in the Bay of Biscay I might as well see what's happening so I defy the Captain's advice and head for the eighth deck (my cabin's on he fifth) where there's a huge restaurant at the front of the ship. By making full use of the hand rails and pausing when we're lifted and dropped by an exceptionally large wave, I make it to the forward part of the 24 hour self-service restaurant. I feel I've climbed a mountain and sit beside the only other passenger in the whole restaurant – a man of a similar age to me. We are sitting where we can look out of the big windows onto the bow of the ship directly below us. It's fantastic. It's like a fairground ride on a big dipper with the same feeling in your stomach every time the ship drops to the ocean. Every so often some crockery and cutlery crashes to the floor in response to a violent motion of the ship. Now and then ocean spray goes right over the top of the ship and obliterates our view through the window. This is so exciting.

Eventually I make my way back to my cabin and manage to get a little fitful sleep.

By morning the storm has subsided.

TRAVELLER'S TIP

Wind it up. The trouble with batteries is they run out of electricity and can leave you up the creek without a paddle (especially in the illumination department).

Why not consider a wind-up head torch? You may look like a miner in search of a shaft but who cares when you have an inexhaustible supply of light to hand? All you have to do is wind the little handle of the internal generator for a couple of minutes to provide you with maybe twenty minutes of light from the LED bulb. It sounds like an outraged mosquito when you're charging up the battery, but again, who cares?

A wind-up radio might also be worth considering.

MOTORCYCLE POWER

From now on I'm taking no notice of the drivers of expensive cars who try to race you at every opportunity.

My Kawasaki motorcycle has a superb one thousand cc engine which develops about 125 brake horse power. The bike weighs about one hundred and eighty kilos which means that its power to weight ratio is quite extraordinary and if I chose to I could beat just about any car on the road.

Some of the expensive car owners see my bike as aggressive and to be beaten (it does have aggressive lines and even when stationary somehow looks as though it's moving at speed!)

Each kilo of my bike's weight is pushed along by almost one and a half brake horse power. That's a heck of a lot of power.

Some of the flash car drivers must be thinking, "Motorcycle, two wheels, inferior. My car cost £60,000 and therefore it must go better than a motorcycle." No! Cash outlay does not in any way relate to your motorcycle-beating properties.

TRAVELLER'S TIP

Always carry a compass. You can get them for next to nothing from camping or walking suppliers or Army surplus stores. Then at least if you get lost you won't be walking in completely the wrong direction.)

YSTAD, SOUTHERN SWEDEN

I'm staying in a hostel a hundred metres from the Baltic Sea. You can hire comfy bicycles by the day which is a great way of exploring the forest walks. The forest goes right up to the sea. It's visually stunning round here, especially now that the brightly coloured leaves are falling from the trees.

I get quite friendly with two Swedish truck drivers who are staying at the hostel. They are transporting timber from the forest in the form of tree trunks to the port of Ystad from where the timber is shipped to Germany. They each have a truck which will carry twenty tonnes and the ship carries a maximum of fourteen hundred tonnes.

I ask the guys the meaning of two Swedish words which have been puzzling me – *slut* and *skum*. It turns out that the first means 'out of order' and the second means 'foam' (I saw it on the side of a fire extinguisher so that makes sense.)

The truck drivers get back to the hostel between eight and ten PM and are up at five to start work at six. They drink lots of strong coffee and take snuff from white circular tins to get themselves going in the mornings.

Ystad, Sweden, Baltic coast.

Ystad, Sweden.

Ystad, Baltic coast.

Ystad, coastal trees.

Ystad, sunset.

One of the guys has a long plaited beard and when at home in Götenburg rides a 1300 cc Harley-Davidson motorcycle. He tells me that for him riding the bike is a relaxation after driving his truck

Ystad.

My Kawasaki Z1000.

all week.

I go to see the piles of timber on the little ship and watch the two o'clock ferry leaving for Poland. A sprinkling of Polish men watch wistfully and no doubt think of their homeland.

Ystad, solitary tree.

There's a strange woman staying at the hostel who never speaks to anyone and only comes out of her room when she thinks no-one is around. She reminds me of a mouse. If she encounters anyone she goes straight back to her room.

I guess she's about sixty and always seems to wear the same blouse.

I surprised her in the corridor one early morning as she was carrying one of the two communal coffee makers to her room for her personal use. She looked decidedly guilty as she scurried past me. Very odd, but it takes all sorts I suppose.

A HAMBURG ART GALLERY

There's a wonderful collection of nineteenth and twentieth century paintings here. Many of them have been restored and the colours are brilliant and clean like they should be, like they once were. It's good to see the pictures like the artists would have liked you to see them, as the artists themselves saw them.

There's a picture of a waterfall. It's fantastic. The white, foaming water crashes and tumbles. You can almost feel the spray on your face.

I talk to the security people. Very few people do. They sit quietly in corners, watching and waiting for their time to be up. They are reflective, silent, inside themselves, but if you talk to them they come to life and become real people with pasts and futures. They like to talk.

I see very many beautiful paintings including Gauguins from his early works through to his mature masterpieces. It's fascinating to see his development. There is one year towards the end of the late 1890's when his art explodes into powerful colour and he finally finds his artistic home. I remember seeing a similar thing in Van Gogh's pictures. In his early work there was a hint of what was to come – I remember a dark painting with just a thin slash of brilliant sunset colours, as though there's a tiny opening in a door through which it has escaped to the darkness from a powerhouse of colour.

Art galleries (good ones, full of works of genius) tire me quickly. I receive so much, but give even more. Forty-five minutes or an hour in the presence of such power is enough. I then need a break before looking at more.

A HAMBURG HOTEL

I talk to the receptionist of Romany people. Both his and my grandmother were of Romany stock. He learnt much more of their ways than I ever have. I tell him of my grandmother's crystal ball, wrapped in its black cloth inside the deep orange-red cylindrical box. My sister has it now. He asked if it worked for her. I say not as far as I know. He said that such gypsy artefacts need their proper homes and can bring bad luck in the wrong hands. I tell him of my own psychic experiences – the ability to feel the presence of spirits, good and bad, and the way I feel their energy down my back – a kind of warm, gentle vibration ... or something cooler and more intense if it's bad. I tell him that I can see pictures in clouds and other abstract things. He says that maybe I should have had the crystal ball and should find out if I can see things in it – that would be the proof.

He says there is one thing that gypsies fear – a curse. Once he was surrounded by five gypsy women out to steal from him. They closed in and he couldn't watch them all. He looked one of them in the eyes and said that he would curse them. They knew he could. They called him offensive names and left him alone. They were frightened.

I told him my grandmother used to read fortunes for the monks at an annual fair. He said he hoped the Abbot never found out or the monks would be for the high jump!

HESTON SERVICE AREA, M4 MOTORWAY

20th October 2009

I'm on my way to visit family in Somerset then on to Devon for a stay at Buckfast Abbey.

I left home (Southend, Essex) at 4.30 am. It's my second long journey on my second-hand Honda Hornet 600 (the first was riding it home from Cornwall, its previous home).

On the whole it's a nice bike. It's white in colour and has fuel injection rather than carburetion like my previous Honda Hornet 600.

My only complaint with it is that you can't adjust the tickover speed. That really irritates me – it's so basic an adjustment. The tickover (which is far too fast) is controlled by the ECU (engine control unit computer I think) and can only be adjusted by Honda dealer mechanics.

I might go back to Kawasaki after this bike – at least you can adjust the tickover speed. In some ways it would be nice to get an old bike where everything is accessible and adjustable. Computer controlled motorcycles are OK as long as everything's working properly.

The SatNav on the other hand is great. If you take a wrong turning it recalculates your route within a few seconds and guides you back on track – which is good because it's very easy to miss turnings in heavy traffic in an unfamiliar city (London). I must have missed five or six turnings but the little device soon got me back on track. The motorcycle ones are fully waterproof.

This is Heston services, the first on the M4. It's small and quite intimate. The coffee place is dimly but adequately lit, the prices are reasonable and the food is good quality. They have comfy armchairs and leather sofas. I had my first coffee there.

I'm now in the other eating place here. It's bright and brash with a TV in the corner (I'm facing away from it deliberately). The tables and chairs are café-like and all the surfaces are hard, which makes for an uncomfortably harsh acoustic.

Going through London by SatNav saved some fifty miles over the M25. It's pretty much a straight along the Thames to the A4 which becomes the M4.

I saw the embankment, the Houses of Parliament, Harrods, went over Tower Bridge and past the big museums in Cromwell Road. It's more interesting than the M25 but your average speed is probably twenty miles per hour at best. On the M25 it would be nearer sixty.

21st October 2009

I'm still here at Heston services. I was too tired to leave yesterday and the sky was dark with impending rain.

Just after midday I went to the Travelodge reception and enquired about a room.

Certainly sir, if you book in now it will be £55 for one night. If you book in after three pm it would be £45."

"Why's that, then?"

"Because we charge a ten pound premium for early occupation."

I don't fancy spending another three hours in the rather depressing eating area.

Breakfast ("continental") here is £4.99, which is pretty good value. It includes a small packet of cereal, a small container of semi-skimmed milk, a small container of orange juice, a croissant, butter pat and portion of marmalade.

Now, to my way of thinking it's not a complete breakfast without coffee or tea. Also, I don't like croissants and would rather have a piece of toast. I made my feelings known to the guy serving the watery tomatoes and sad sausages. He saw my point but was unable to make a decision without the agreement of his supervisor. He called her over and explained my position. She agreed I could have toast but not a free coffee so I had to pay an extra £2.10 for the smallest Americano.

I was annoyed so I took a big handful of the new kind of milk sachets (which you have to milk like a cow to get anything out of them) and a handful of sugars for my emergency supply at home.

TRAVELLER'S TIP

Take a favourite book with you. Then when you come across a traveller's shelf of books exchange yours for another. If you do this you may find a fantastic book that you'd never have found in any other way. All you have to do is keep your mind open to other people's choices. Expect some surprises.

MOROCCO, December 2015

MARRAKECH MUSICIANS

Today I watched two groups of musicians in the main square.

The first seemed a little more professional. Four drummers, two voices. I closed my eyes and listened to ancient music. The big drum throbbed. The voices rose and fell and intertwined like quickly-growing plants.

It was mesmeric, dark and sexual.

A fine-looking man with a black beard, a red shirt under a striped djellabah and a green hat darted quickly amongst the crowd collecting money.

The other band had the feel of being semi-professional. A couple of them seemed too clean, too perfect. They were both immaculately dressed – one in Western clothes, the other in Arab dress.

The band comprised three drummers (of which two were also singers) and a banjo player. The sound of the banjo blended perfectly with the three different types of drum – one bass, one middle, one high.

They were a very tight outfit and played what I imagine were traditional Berber songs, many with choruses where all the musicians joined in.

This band was competent but lacked the dark sexual tension of the other band.

TRAFFIC

It's surprising there aren't corpses and badly injured pedestrians lying around all over the place in Marrakech.

Driving, as well as cycling and being a pedestrian is the art of avoiding contact by a gnat's whisker.

It's not a stop/start thing like in other countries – cars, motorcycles, buses, cyclists and pedestrians are in a constant state of flux, a dance almost, weaving in and out of each others paths and coming within a few inches of hitting each other, but never quite doing so. It makes no difference really where you cross the road – on a pedestrian crossing or not – the traffic behaves the same way wherever you happen to be.

The thing is, the system works well and because of the dangers, it means that drivers and pedestrians alike are super vigilant … that's why it's really rather safe.

Tomorrow I'm hiring a car for a week or so to drive to Essaouira amongst other places as yet undecided. I shall find out first hand what it's like to almost drive into other traffic and almost run down pedestrians.

MONKEYS

I feel sorry for the monkeys of Marrakech, dressed in their frilly yellow frocks and red cotton shorts trained to do somersaults at the end of a leash (without a leash they would surely try to run back to their natural environment) and to sit on tourists' shoulders so photographs can be taken.

Yesterday I saw a monkey sitting on a male tourist's shoulder. His wife reached out to try to shake the monkey's hand but it had suffered enough indignity for one day and tried to bite the woman's hand. I hope its teeth made contact with her flesh. If I was one of those monkeys I'd try to bite as many tourists as possible to show the way I felt about my predicament.

CROSSING THE ROAD

I've discovered the safest way to cross a busy road in Marrakech is to make sure there are other pedestrians between you and the approaching traffic. You let them make decisions about when to walk out in front of cars then you follow their moves exactly, always making sure they remain between you and the traffic. That way, if a car does mow some of them down you'll most likely be shielded by them and should escape injury.

ESSAOUIRA, MOROCCO

I've only been here an hour but already there are signs that this place lives up to its reputation of being an old hippy colony – the likes of Jimi Hendrix and Cat Stevens came here in the 60's to sort out their heads (or perhaps to make them more muddled).

After the car park guy the first person I met was a street hassler who claimed it was his job to escort me to my residence. He had a deep, liquid cough that spoke of the consumption of countless kilos of hashish over the years. After walking me around for a few minutes we arrived at the agents for Jack's Apartments where I'm staying.

He demanded five dollars (approximately thirty Moroccan deram) for helping me find the agents. I ended up giving him twenty deram just to get rid of him. As we parted company he said in a deep, dark voice,

"If you need any drugs you've only got to find me. I'll be able to get you what you want."

I assured him I had no need for anything like that. My dope smoking days are long past.

I have one of the cheaper apartments without a sea view (the block is right next to the Atlantic Ocean), but if you go on the roof terrace, four floors above beach level, there are all the sea views anyone could possibly need.

The apartment itself is newly-converted, clean and well designed. It's open plan on a small scale with a separate toilet area and shower area. The TV has numerous satellite channels but I doubt if any of them will be in English.

Outside the apartment and just down the passage there's a rather fine shared kitchen area. Again, newly-converted with, it would seem, pretty much everything in the way of crockery, cutlery and utensils needed to eat breakfast or cook an evening meal. Next stop, a supermarket.

Essaouira is overrun with beggars. I read somewhere that a good way of dealing with them and at the same time salving your conscience is to give one beggar a day a reasonable amount (in Morocco say a ten deram coin) then just say 'no' to all the others. I've been trying it out and it works a treat for me and I don't feel a tinge of guilt.

When a beggar approaches with outstretched hand I understand there's an Arabic expression you can use which means 'I'm sorry but today I have already given.' It's an expression which satisfies them and I gather they immediately turn away from you and approach someone else.

I'm getting rather irritated by all the crass, hippy-inspired bits of advice that have been stencilled onto walls and ceilings of Jack's Apartments. Things like,

Be so happy that when someone looks at you they become happy

too.

Or,

Some people look for a beautiful place. Others make a place beautiful.

Or,

Sometimes you will never know the value of a moment until it becomes a memory.

And other such nonsense.

I used to be quite open to hippy ideas (back in the 1960's and '70's) when they seemed to point towards a new way of living ... but now I realise those sentiments often had no more weight or substance than candy floss.

You don't realise how big seagulls are till you see them close up. The ones that hang around this apartment block let you get within a few feet before they take flight on their magnificent wings.

I'm on the roof terrace and I can hear the Atlantic breakers pushing towards the sharp and stubborn rock outcrop below. Water pounds into the rock and white spray rises high and is blown sideways by the wind.

Yesterday in the desert landscape beside the highway between Marrakech and Essaouira for the first time in my life I saw mesas and butts. I remembered them from school geography and was quite excited to see those hard rock desert outcrops for real.

I guess the little rock islands I can see now from the terrace are the marine equivalents.

Chunky Coyte the geography master taught me well, as did Mr Dean who once in a while used to make the most beautiful coloured chalk drawings of geographical features on the blackboard in his lunch hour only to wipe them out of existence at the end of the lesson. They were real works of art and all the more beautiful for being rare and transient like desert flowers.

I wonder how many ships have been wrecked on those razor-sharp rocks. The powerful, turbulent sea has done its best to smooth them but they are sharp to the core.

Close up, the rocks are like pinkish, weathered bone.

The breakers rise, tumble, crash and foam. Their sound is deep and massive.

The nearest land to this bit of West African coast is North America.

TRAVELLER'S TIP

Take clothing and shoes that will serve more than one purpose. Pay particular attention to what shoes you take away with you. I bought a fantastic pair of black lace-up shoes in Brisbane. They were really cheap and they don't make your feet smell, even in the hot weather. They're extremely light in weight and the uppers are made of a shiny synthetic material which looks just like leather and you can bring them back to a perfect shine with the wipe of a damp cloth. I wore them all day and went out in the evenings in them too.

Long sleeved shirts are very handy and multi-purpose too (especially ones that protect you from the sun's rays) – You can wear the sleeves down or rolled up and give them an iron if you want to look a bit special in the evening (with your plastic shoes).

As for trousers – camping shops sell trousers which convert into shorts if you unzip the legs. They're pretty useful.

PARIS

I got up to some ridiculous speeds on the *péage* (pay road) to Paris on my Honda Hornet 600. That was exciting.

In Paris I chanced upon the Hôtel 7th Art, only five minutes walk from Nôtre Dame. It's near La Place de Bastille just off the Rue Saint Paul.

Monsieur Jean the owner offered me a pretty good room at the top of the hotel for €65 a night.

At night I can hear a strange deep vibration but I've got use to it now. I guess it's some kind of fan or maybe something to do with the central heating.

Paris at night

Eiffel Tower

Interior of the Hôtel 7th Art, Paris.

Monsieur Jean is great. He has a lovely lyrical voice and is humorous, mischievous and a fount of knowledge.

Louvre Fountain.

"You need a purple shirt, Monsieur? Then you need to go to BHV (pronounced bay-aasha-vay in French).

I made my way to the BHV store and encountered two Arabs in

yellow hats selling shirts on the pavement more or less outside the store. I bought two shirts from them, a purple one and a red one for €5 each.

When I got back I told Monsieur Jean,

"J'ai acheté deux chemises sur le trottoir. Ils sont très jolie, n'est-ce pas?" ("I bought two shirts on the pavement. They're rather attractive, don't you think?")

"Mais oui!" exclaimed Monsieur Jean.

Monsieur Jean is like a fish out of water today. He is unable to inhabit the security of his reception desk because electricians are fitting a new alarm system. He doesn't know what to do with himself and stands around awkwardly.

Monsieur Jean is a man with a wonderful obsession. He has given his little hotel a film theme and the care he has put into the detail is admirable. The menus have a Laurel and Hardy theme, the reception area is richly decorated with movie posters and the breakfast area is festooned with miniature projection equipment and movie cameras.

OUISTREM CAMPSITE, Northern France

I need a plug for the washbasins. I prepare myself well with the aid of the dictionary and come up with a sentence I'm very proud of.

"Une question, Madame. J'ai besoin d'une ventouse pour les lavabos. S'il vous plâit, où j'achete cette chose? (I have a question, dear lady. I need a suction pad for the washbasins. Where might I purchase such an object, please?)

My French grammar may not be perfect, but I consider it a pretty fine question nonetheless by someone who barely scraped a pass in his 'O' Level French and was almost struck dumb during the oral examination.

My question is immediately answered by the woman in the campsite reception office and she tells me they are available in supermarkets.

It's very satisfying to ask a question of a foreigner in their own language and to be understood. The problem comes when they assume you must be fluent in their language and reply with a rushing torrent of foreign words which might as well be Greek as far as you are concerned (or may in fact be Greek). This onslaught may go on for several minutes during which time you pretend to understand by nodding vigorously and throwing in an occasional 'yes' in their language. At the end of the encounter you will of course be absolutely none the wiser about anything.

PORTO, PORTUGAL

Almeida Garret Park, Porto.

Balconies, Porto.

Portuguese tiles.

The Portuguese cafés are not crazy, gabbling places like the Spanish ones. They are relaxed, quiet, easy places where your

Porto main railway station.

personal space and right to peace and quiet are respected. You can get six or eight people, all on their own, all self-absorbed in reading or watching TV or looking out of the window. You are left to your own devices.

THE PORTUGUESE TRAFFIC GAME

A Porto park.

Red maple leaves, a Porto park.

A game the Portuguese play is to see how close you can get to dying in a traffic accident.

In the city it's practiced at professional level.

On just about every corner is a pedestrian crossing. Pedestrians have right of way but the vehicle drivers want that little bit of space every bit as badly as the walking folk and there is a constant battle between the two.

If you wait patiently by the roadside for the traffic to stop you'll be disappointed and never get across. You have to act boldly, which means stepping out with confidence yet with a degree of nonchalance in front of rapidly approaching traffic. It's imperative to show that you mean business. If you step out with confidence the traffic *will* stop. If you hesitate it won't. The last thing those drivers want to do is stop to let you cross. You've just got to show them who's boss. If you don't they'll weave round you and you'll probably find yourself retreating to the safety of the pavement.

In just about every case the driver will stop before he reaches the crossing, but if he doesn't, at least from your hospital bed you'll have the satisfaction of knowing that he'll be facing a very severe penalty which should make you feel a bit better.

THE PORTUGUESE LOOKING GAME

This is a great game you can play whenever you're walking on the street. You play it with people who are walking towards you.. There's only one rule and the rule is, "I'll look at you until our eyes meet then I'll look away and you can look at me for a while." It's a very civilised game.

This rule may work in other countries too – it's worth a try. It certainly won't work in Turkey where the men continue to stare no matter how long you stare back. Also, it's best not to try this game in the UK – it will only cause huge embarrassment to those you look at and the natives could become aggressive and dangerous.

THE PORTUGUESE SHOP GAME

Sometimes when you go in a shop or supermarket the shopkeeper or cashier will be deep in conversation with a customer. Don't expect them to rapidly bring matters to a conclusion for your benefit. They won't. They'll carry on as if you're not there for as long as it takes, and that can be several minutes. Just when you think it's tailing off and they're about to wrap things up and you step forward, they'll start up again with renewed vigour.

In this situation it's best to retreat to a respectful distance and wait quietly and patiently until they're done. If you start shifting about impatiently and muttering under your breath like you might do in your own country they'll find something else to talk about just to make you suffer for a bit longer.

Best to be philosophical about it and accept it as a small tile in the colourful mosaic of Portuguese life.

TRAVELLER'S TIP

As you wander in a strange town or city, at every junction look back to the way you've come and imprint the image on your mind. Better still, take photos. That way you'll more easily be able to find your way back. Things look different when you're going in the opposite direction.

ROSTRENEN, BRITTANY, FRANCE, August 2018

I arrived at Dunkirk by ferry from Dover. It was the cheapest option but I grossly miscalculated what I'd spend on petrol and road tolls. It's about a thousand kilometres from Dunkirk to Rostrenen where I've taken Airbnb rooms in a beautiful old house. The toll roads alone cost about fifty pounds and I don't even want to work out what the petrol has cost so far but wouldn't be surprised if it's approaching two hundred pounds. It was a false economy paying a hundred and nine pounds for the ferry.

I drove for almost ten hours to get from Dunkirk to this wonderful house. It's owned and run by a lovely lady called Annie who lives about half an hour away.

The house is about a hundred and twenty years old and the first floor has been converted into three large bedrooms. The smallest has its own kitchen and shares a bathroom with the middle room (which also has its own kitchen). I have the best room with its own bathroom and kitchen adjacent to each other.

Downstairs is a large communal seating area which looks out onto the garden. The room has twenty-four seats and five tables. There is also a large kitchen and a massage therapy room with purple wallpaper. I had a massage yesterday with a lovely lady called Pascale. She swung a pendulum over me before the massage and

Annie with her two dogs

Identified two areas of ill health – my chest and my solar plexus. She wasn't far wrong – I have a lung disease called pulmonary fibrosis and am bipolar (which is kind of rooted in the solar plexus – that's where the feelings of depression and mania originate).

The two dogs

The massage was lovely and the music exquisite – it was a CD by Steve Halpern called *Radiance (Love Songs Without Words)* which came out in 1989 but is timeless stuff. It lasts almost exactly one hour which was the length of the massage.

Me in front of a huge red cedar in the magical garden

This house is quiet, spacious and peaceful and has a massive garden with huge red cedar trees, the tallest of which must be well over a hundred feet. They are as straight as dies. It takes you several minutes to walk to the other end of the garden where Annie told me that sometimes roe deer wander. Near the house are several tables and chairs and a barbeque area.

The house through the trees

I'm the only guest here. The front door is always unlocked (although I lock my room when I go out) and the shower is the best one I've ever used. I have the run of this fantastic house and all for twenty-three pounds a night!

A few days ago was the wedding of my friends Robert and Sue. It was fascinating to attend a French wedding ceremony which was conducted by the female deputy mayor. There was a translator present who translated the whole service from French into English.

The back of Robert and Sue with the deputy mayor (right) and the translator in the background

After the happy couple were married two poems were read out (poetry is very much part of their lives and Robert is a brilliant poet) and I produced one that I just happened to have in my bag by an Indian woman, Mona Arshi, called *What Every Girl Should Know Before Marriage* and was very funny. The last line was, *"Your husband may not know you cheated with shop-bought garam masala but God will know."*

After I'd read it out the translator said that she was legally obliged to translate it into French. I gave her the poem and wished her good luck. She made a magnificent job of it, given that she was completely unprepared for the translation and poetry can't be the easiest form to translate. When she finished the wedding guests gave her a huge round of applause.

All the guests repaired to the house of the bride and groom (who have lived together for thirty years) in Le Bout Du Pont (which is in the commune of Plélauff). Sue told me that the main reason for their marriage was that if she dies Robert will inherit her pension for the rest of his life, but only if they are married.

A guy played acoustic guitar and I accompanied him on Robert's C blues harmonica (I forgot to take my harmonicas with me) when he played a couple of blues numbers he had written.

I had an interesting time talking to the wedding guests, especially

Sue's son Mathew. His Japanese wife Sukia and their lovely daughter Otternay (whose name was invented by Sukia and is part Japanese, part Chinese and means 'music of the Universe').

A French lady from the village where she has lived all her life.

Later we all went to a restaurant a few miles away run by an English couple for fish and chips and wedding cake. There were about twenty of us.

All in all it was a fantastic day.

A metal horse sculpture at Rostrenen

The same beautiful horse sculpture, Rostrenen

Today (Sunday) I went to L'abbaye de bon repos (The abbey of agreeable rest), which is near Gouarec, a few miles from where I'm staying in Rostrenen. It used to house Cistercian monks and was abandoned during the French Revolution in 1799.

Now it's a fascinating tourist attraction.

The dreams exhibition at L'abbaye de Bon Repos, Gouarec

There was an exhibition relating to dreams and a shop which sold fossils and jewellery. There was another shop which sold French books. I bought an address book because mine has worn out and a few people who have died need to be deleted from my life. From the fossil shop I bought a trilobite from Brittany and two fossils of small squids which are between three hundred and four hundred million years old. I gave one of them to Robert and Sue.

My black Peugeot 207 1400 cc petrol car enjoyed it in its home country and knew what to do at roundabouts. It's eleven years old and has done just 64,000 miles. It's a great little car and is well capable of a hundred and ten miles an hour or more. It's got a couple of irritating faults – there's a misfire when the engine's cold and a seat belt warning sounds randomly, which is extremely irritating (it gets louder and louder till you take notice of it). Also, the key won't always unlock the door. I hope it doesn't fail completely but if it does I'll just have to unlock the door manually.

Someone told me on another French visit a few years ago that if you greatly exceed the speed limit on the toll roads, that if you stop at a rest area for fifteen or twenty minutes it will bring your average speed right down. Advice I always follow.

Printed in Poland
by Amazon Fulfillment
Poland Sp. z o.o., Wrocław

54550693R00074